MW00677883

The Glocap Guide To

Getting A Job In
Private Equity

Behind The Scenes Insight Into How PE Funds Hire

Case Studies   Insider Tips   Resumes

Brian Korb and Glocap's Private Equity Team

GLOCAP

Design and layout: Levine Design, Cambridge, MA

Address:
156 W. 56th
NY, NY 10019

ISBN 0-9777929-0-0

Printed in the United States of America

Table of Contents

Charts

Case Studies

Resumes

Introduction

When we sat down to write this guide our goal was to paint an accurate picture of career prospects in the private equity industry. We wanted to excite people about the industry and encourage them to pursue their dream job. At the same time, however, we didn't want to give anyone false hopes. For most people finding a position in private equity will be very difficult. The number of candidates pursuing private equity jobs has always far outpaced the number of available positions. Perhaps never before has the private equity profession wielded such power or played as important a role in the financial markets as it does at present. The appeal is obvious: private equity is about buying and controlling companies, and in today's market some of those are among the largest in the world. Private equity investors work with companies from the initial investment to the time they are taken public or sold. They grow and nurture them and ultimately determine their fate by taking board seats and exerting influence on operations and strategy. They are passionate about investing and have the ability to create millions (even billions) of dollars of value.

If you've already looked into getting a position at a private equity fund, you may have been warned that the challenge could be significant and the competition fierce. This guide will give you a better understanding of the career path in private equity and how hiring works. However, we do not profess to offer sure-fire, can't-miss strategies for getting a job, because there aren't any! Remember, as in other industries, there are timing issues and natural business cycles that are out of your control. Our aim is to give you insight into the elements that are in your control so you can put your best foot forward during your pursuit of a job. This guide also does not take a textbook look at private equity, give a detailed history of the industry or explain how funds are raised and deals are done. You can get that information from many other sources (some of which we point out in the Appendix).

We segment candidates looking for positions in private equity by where they are in their professional careers and thus have chapters on the most common entry points: out of undergrad, from an investment banking or consulting Analyst program (these are typical initial feeders into private equity jobs as you will see later), from business school and post graduate school. We also devote a separate chapter to venture capital (earlier-stage investing) because the skill sets venture funds look for, the timing of the opportunities to break in and the career track all differ significantly from later-stage private equity funds. For this guide we will focus primarily on junior and senior (non-Partner) roles at mid- and later-stage private equity and leveraged buyout (LBO) funds. When we use the traditional term private equity (PE), we are referring to the entire spectrum of early- to later-stage investing. If we are discussing a specific portion of the market, for example venture capital or buyouts, we will note it by name.

Most people target a long-term career in private equity by following what we call the "traditional path." This is also called the "2-2-2" route because it usually involves spending two years each in an Analyst training program (investment banking or consulting), a PE firm and then business school before securing a career-track opportunity. As you read this guide, you will learn that it is very hard to go back in the process and make up for missed experiences. If you didn't land in an investment banking or consulting Analyst program after undergrad it will be difficult to secure a pre-MBA position at a PE/LBO fund and if you wake up one day in business school (or later on) and have an epiphany that PE is for you but you lack prior PE experience the battle is likely to be even more challenging. We will outline the traditional path and refer to it throughout this guide, but, it is not the *only* way to get into PE. There are people who get in other ways and we will give attention to them.

Real-Life Stories

This is a dynamic time for the private equity industry. Fundraising continues to break records, deals are plentiful (and getting larger and larger as evidenced by very recent activity) and hiring continues to be strong. As recruiters who specialize in PE we are in a unique position to offer job search advice: we know what the PE firms demand and we are intimately aware of the experiences of candidates who have successfully found jobs. However, in addition to our own guidance we believe a great way for you to *really* get a grasp of the private equity search process is to read insight from people on both sides of the spectrum who have experienced it first hand. For the hiring firms, we have insight (Insider Tips) from PE professionals, some of whom are in positions to make hiring decisions. Some will tell you how they got where they are, others will offer tips into what they look for when hiring. There is also a healthy dose of warnings about potential pitfalls to avoid.

On the candidate side, we have first-hand accounts (Case Studies) of 27 people who went through the search process and we have included resumes from 15 of them. The experiences outlined in the Case Studies run the gamut from people who broke into PE the more traditional way to ones who lacked the usual requirements but were still able to secure a position. We have Case Studies from pre-MBAs, current MBAs and people up to several years out of graduate school. What the authors of all the Case Studies have in common is that they were top performers both academically and professionally and had a burning desire to succeed. By reading the Case Studies you will see quickly that, in most instances, to secure a job in private equity you must be willing to commit early, put in the work, get the best education/training and do whatever else it takes to excel—and that's true whether you eventually break in via the traditional or non-traditional path. Are we saying that many of you can find a position without the traditional background? No, but if you follow the advice of those that were the exceptions, have a stellar background and are willing to work hard, you can improve your chances to be an exception as well. We are grateful to all those people who shared their stories and resumes with us.

At times we will use professional sports analogies to describe various aspects of the job market. We believe the competitiveness, intensity, pace and even the potential for compensation in the private equity industry parallels the sports world. In fact, sports terms are commonly used by private equity professionals so you may find being familiar with them a useful asset going forward. For example, funds hiring at the more senior level may tell us they are looking for someone who can "quarterback" a deal. When targeting junior level staff, the same funds say they want people who can "block and tackle" for their deal teams. Mid-market funds often want "utility fielders" who can take on a lot of roles given that they are smaller, less structured organizations.

We view the process of finding a job in private equity as similar to that of reaching the Major Leagues in baseball, the NFL or the NBA, etc. and, thus, as someone striving to make it into PE, we think you should tackle your search in the same way as someone training to be a pro athlete. To succeed in either athletics or private equity you need to have a high-level of natural ability and work overtime to make up for areas in which you are deficient. In baseball, if a pitcher can't throw a 90 mile-per-hour fastball he will have a tough time making it to the Majors. And, even if he *can* throw 90 mph there is no guarantee he will make it. This guide will help you reduce the chances of that happening. Think of working in private equity as your Major Leagues, it's where the big money and the big contracts are. You may have everything that it takes to eventually work in private equity, but for a variety of reasons could still find yourself on the short end of the stick. If you want to be a big earner and a superstar in this industry, you are going to have to do the work to get there, but you will have to do the right work. Anyone can work hard. Getting ahead in PE is about working smart and getting on track early. We wish you luck!

chapter I

Private Equity 101

Before initiating your job search, there are a few things about private equity with which you should be thoroughly familiar. Even if you think you know the nuts and bolts, this chapter could serve as a brush-up on PE basics, including how various funds and roles differ. The people who interview you will expect you to know these things. If you don't know them you risk sounding unprepared and there is no room for that in private equity. Finally, we will also explain some basic employment terms that we will use throughout the rest of this guide.

While we want to avoid sounding like a textbook, we still think it is important to discuss the basics of what PE funds are and how they are structured. A "Private Equity Fund" may sound like it would be a stand-alone entity, but it usually is not. Even though people say they are an Analyst or Senior Associate at fund ABC, they really work for a management company that has a fee agreement with the actual fund. For example, Chicago-based Madison Dearborn Partners, LLC is the management company for funds including the Madison Dearborn Capital Partners III, L.P. ($2.2 billion), the Madison Dearborn Capital Partners IV, L.P. ($4 billion) and the Madison Dearborn Capital Partners V, L.P.; a $6.5 billion investment fund raised in 2006. Most PE funds are set up as Limited Partnerships. As such, they have a General Partner (GP) in charge of making decisions for the partnership and Limited Partners (LPs) who are the investors in the fund. Typical LPs are institutional investors including public and private pension funds, endowments, other large financial institutions, wealthy individuals and the Partners of the fund themselves.

The GPs make money two different ways: through an annual management fee paid by the investors in the fund (the LPs) and a carried interest ("carry")—a percent of profit paid to the General Partner. The annual management fee is usually 1.5-2.5% of total capital commitments to the fund, while the carry has been historically 20% of profits. You will often hear the term "2 and 20" to describe this fee structure. That means a $1 billion fund with a 2% management fee will take in $20 million in fees each year to pay salaries and overhead. If the fund doubles over the course of its lifetime, to $2 billion (a 100% profit), the management company will reap $200 million based on an incentive fee of 20% with that sum split among the Partners and anyone else with a piece of carry at the fund. A very select group of venture capital or leveraged buyout firms can even take home 25% to 30% of profits. Don't get ahead of yourself here, if you join in a junior role you will not likely get a large percentage of the carry, but some of it can filter down to you.

And, if you stay on for several years you can be in a position to build real wealth as your percentage grows significantly (see Chapter XII for a more detailed discussion on compensation).

Characteristics Of Private Equity Investments

In its simplest form, a private equity investment is a privately negotiated transaction involving an equity ownership stake. By their nature private equity investments are less correlated to the public equity markets and are also less subject to stock market cycles. PE funds can offer the possibility of greater returns than investing in public equities, but these investments are also relatively illiquid. So if an investment in a fund is turning south it's not easy to exit. Although many of the large LBOs that have made headlines over the past several years were buyouts of public companies (if a public company is taken over entirely it is what is known as "going private"), PE funds most often invest in private companies whose stock is not listed on a public exchange.

What The Funds Do

Throughout your interview process you will be asked numerous times why you want to work in PE. The basis for your answer lies in understanding exactly what funds do. A PE fund earns its money based on the appreciation of its equity in the operating companies in which it invests. Of course, not all investments lead to profits. A typical $1 billion fund will make multiple investments, and, while some may not produce profits, a few large successes could be enough to provide significant returns for the entire fund.

The vast majority of investment professionals' time and effort at PE funds is spent making investments, which includes finding, reviewing, evaluating, negotiating and structuring deals. Once investments are made many funds dedicate a significant amount of time to monitoring and adding value to portfolio companies before exiting the investment. Generally, PE funds buy controlling or highly influential interests in companies. This element of control/influence is an essential ingredient in funds' ability to add value to their investments. PE firms add value multiple ways:

- Provide capital and guidance in the form of financial strategies to grow the company
- Actively guide operational strategy
- Help make add-on acquisitions to grow the company
- Sell various (sometimes non-essential) parts of a business
- Replace management and/or restructure operations if necessary

The typical cycle for a PE fund is:

- Raise money from investors (LPs)
- Invest that money in operating companies
- Use a pre-determined strategy to add value to the company
- Exit (sell) the investment
- Split the profit with investors (LPs)

The Different Types Of Funds

Knowing the various funds/investment types will help you understand the industry and determine where you want to work and, just as relevant, the best fit for your skills. There are several types of PE funds. The main factor that separates them is the stage of a company's life at which a fund invests. As stated earlier, this guide will focus primarily on mid- to later-stage PE, which includes leveraged buyout (LBO) and growth equity funds. We also include a chapter on early-stage venture capital (VC). Some firms may have multiple funds. For example, Bain Capital has both venture capital and LBO funds.

BUYOUT FUNDS

Leveraged buyout or simply "buyout funds," invest in more mature, later-stage companies that are almost always cash flow positive. As their name suggests, LBO funds purchase, or buy out, an entire company or a controlling interest in a corporation's equity. LBOs are structured using a combination of debt and equity. The word "leverage" indicates that debt is used to leverage the fund's equity investment, allowing for a larger total purchase (and related larger financial return). In a similar fashion, a mortgage allows for the purchase of a larger home then would straight equity (a down payment).

We separate LBO funds into large and middle-market funds. Large funds (which include what we call mega-funds with several billion dollars in assets under management) typically invest in multi-billion dollar transactions often through an auction process (run by investment banks) and can do so in partnership with other large funds if the deal size warrants it. Middle-market funds (typically $1 billion and less) invest in smaller deals and look to source those deals through proprietary relationships.

CHART 1
Largest Buyout Funds Ever Raised (as of 12/31/2006)

Rank	Fund Name	Firm Name	Location	Year	Amount ($Bln)
1	KKR 2006 Fund LP*	Kohlberg Kravis Roberts & Co.	New York	2006	$16.10
2	Blackstone Capital Partners V LP*	Blackstone Group	New York	2006	$15.60
3	TPG Partners V LP	Texas Pacific Group Inc.	Fort Worth, Texas	2006	$15.00
4	Permira IV	Permira Advisers LLP	London	2006	$13.8**
5	Apollo Investment Fund VI LP	Apollo Advisors LP	New York	2005	$10.00
	Bain Capital IX LP + coinvestment fund	Bain Capital	Boston	2006	$10.00
7	GS Capital Partners V LP	GS Capital Partners Inc.	New York	2005	$8.50
8	Fourth Cinven Fund	Cinven Ltd.	London	2006	$8.10
9	Warburg Pincus Private Equity IX LP	Warburg Pincus LLC	New York	2005	$8.00
10	Carlyle Partners	Carlyle Group	Washington	2005	$7.90
11	First Reserve Fund XI LP	First Reserve Corp.	Greenwich, CT	2006	$7.80
12	CVC European Partners IV LP	CVC Capital Partners	London	2005	$7.5**
13	Providence Equity Partners VI LP*	Providence Equity Partners Inc.	Providence, R.I.	2006	$7.00
14	BC European Capital VIII	BC Partners	London	2005	$6.8*
15	GS Infrastructure Partners	GS Capital Partners Inc.	New York	2006	$6.50
	JPMorgan Partners Global Investors	CCMP Capital Advisors LLC	New York	2002	$6.50
	Madison Dearborn, Capital Partners V LP	Madison Dearborn Partners LLC	Chicago	2006	$6.50

Source: Dow Jones Private Equity Analyst
* Fund still open as of early 2007. **Converted from euros using 2005 currency averages

- Some of the noteworthy firms that have larger buyout funds are Apollo Management; Bain Capital; The Blackstone Group; Carlyle Group; GS Capital Partners; Kohlberg Kravis Roberts; Madison Dearborn Partners; Permira Advisers; Providence Equity Partners; Texas Pacific Group; Thomas H. Lee Partners and Warburg Pincus.

- Examples of firms that have mid-market buyout funds are Aurora Capital Group; Brazos Private Equity Partners; Brentwood Associates; Bruckmann Rosser Sherril; Centre Partners; Charlesbank Capital Partners; Fremont Partners; Genstar Capital; H.I.G. Capital; KRG Capital Partners and Wind Point Partners.

VENTURE CAPITAL FUNDS

Venture capital funds are very different than LBO funds; not only in how they invest, but also how they hire, pay and promote their investment professionals (we will discuss this more in Chapter VIII). In brief, venture capital funds invest in companies that are not yet producing cash: in fact, they are often cash flow negative or "burning cash." VC funds almost always invest in companies before they are profitable, often before they have revenue and sometimes even before they have a product. Venture funds are looking for the next great product or company that will revolutionize a specific industry. VC funds usually target industries within information technology (including semiconductors, Internet and software), healthcare (biotech, medical devices and healthcare services) and increasingly clean technology, with some funds targeting all three areas. For example, Kleiner Perkins Caufield & Byers, one of the original backers of Google, invests in technology components, systems and software as well as in healthcare.

- Firms with VC funds include Battery Ventures; Benchmark Capital; Bessemer Venture Partners; Charles River Ventures; Draper Fisher Jurvetson; Greylock Partners; Kleiner Perkins; Menlo Ventures; New Enterprise Associates; The Mayfield Fund; Sutter Hill Ventures and Sequoia Capital.

GROWTH EQUITY FUNDS

Whereas venture capital funds target early-stage companies and LBO funds seek out more mature, profitable and cash-producing businesses, growth equity funds invest in companies that lie somewhere in between. Specifically, these companies are more mature than those in which venture funds invest. Growth equity funds target companies that are usually profitable or close to it. They generally have proven business models but may need capital to grow. Transactions done by growth equity funds less frequently involve leverage (as many of these growing businesses have yet to amass the assets and/or are not producing enough cash against which to borrow). The transactions usually involve purchasing significant ownership (but not necessarily full-control) in portfolio companies.

- Some larger, well-known examples of firms with growth equity funds are General Atlantic Partners; Spectrum Equity Investors; Summit Partners and TA Associates.

Other Funds

While this guide will not spend significant time discussing other types of PE-related funds, such as Mezzanine, Funds of Funds and Secondary Funds we do offer a brief outline. These funds differ from the PE funds mentioned earlier because they do not invest directly into businesses and/or do not involve equity. They can all be great paths to pursue when seeking an investment job, but they require a different skill set and involve substantially different investment styles than the traditional PE funds.

CHART 2
Largest Venture Capital Funds Ever Raised *(as of 12/31/2006)*

Rank	Fund Name	Firm Name	Location	Year	Amount ($Bln)
1	Oak Investment Partners XII	Oak Investment Partners	Westport, Conn.	2006	$2.56
2	New Enterprise Associates XII LP	New Enterprise Associates	Baltimore	2006	$2.50
3	New Enterprise Associates X LP	New Enterprise Associates	Baltimore	2000	$2.30
4	Spectrum Equity Investors IV LP	Spectrum Equity Investors	Boston	2001	$2.00
5	Technology Crossover Ventures IV LP	Technology Crossover Ventures	Palo Alto, Calif.	2000	$1.70
6	VantagePoint Venture Partners IV LP	VantagePoint Venture Partners	San Bruno, Calif.	2000	$1.61
7	Oak Investment Partners X LP	Oak Investment Partners	Westport, Conn.	2001	$1.60
8	Oak Investment Partners XI LP	Oak Investment Partners	Westport, Conn.	2004	$1.50
	Softbank Capital Partners LP	Softbank Capital	Newton Center, Mass.	1999	$1.50
	Menlo Ventures IX LP	Menlo Ventures	Menlo Park, Calif.	2000	$1.50
11	Technology Crossover Ventures VI LP	Technology Crossover Ventures	Palo Alto, Calif.	2005	$1.40
12	Weston Presidio Capital IV LP	Weston Presidio Capital	Boston	2000	$1.37
13	Mobius Technology Ventures VI LP	Mobius Venture Capital Inc.	Palo Alto, Calif.	2000	$1.25
14	Menlo Ventures X LP	Menlo Ventures	Menlo Park, Calif.	2005	$1.20

Source: Dow Jones: Private Equity Analyst

MEZZANINE FUNDS

Mezzanine funds invest in private debt (i.e., mezzanine debt) frequently into LBO deals. This can come from private and/or public sources and can invest in public or private companies. Mezzanine debt is the middle layer of debt used in leveraged buyouts—subordinated to the senior debt layer but above the equity layer. This type of hybrid structure often incorporates equity-based options, such as warrants, with a lower-priority debt. Mezzanine debt is often used to finance buyouts where it can be give new owners priority over existing ones in the event of a bankruptcy.

Mezzanine level financing can take the form of preferred stock or convertible bonds. It can also provide late (bridge) financing for venture-backed companies immediately prior to a company's IPO. In some cases people who have worked at mezzanine funds have moved into PE funds, but that is often an exception. In addition, some well-known firms—GTCR in Chicago and Audax Group in Boston for instance—have both mezzanine and PE funds, so some people's roles can involve both types of investing.

- A few firms with mezzanine funds are: Capital Resources Partners; Northstar Capital Partners and Peninsula Capital Partners.

FUND OF FUNDS

Fund of funds invest in a selection of PE funds rather than directly in operating companies. They are a way for some investors, particularly smaller institutions, high-net-worth individuals or family offices, to diversify their PE investment risk. By investing in dozens of PE funds, a fund of funds could have indirect exposure to hundreds of companies. Fund of funds can also have many more LPs. Because the skills are so different, working at a fund of funds is usually not considered a stepping stone to working at an LBO shop.

- Well-known managers of private equity fund of funds include Adam Street Partners; AlpInvest Partners; HarbourVest Partners and Horsley Bridge Partners.

SECONDARY FUNDS

Secondary funds purchase part or all of an interest in an existing PE Fund. For example, Pension Fund A may have invested $50 million in LBO Fund I two years ago and now decides that it doesn't want to be an investor in LBO Fund I. Secondary Fund X comes in and offers Pension Fund A $35 million for its $50 million interest in LBO Fund I. Pension Fund A sells its interest in LBO Fund I with the consent of the PE fund. The valuation that takes place in secondary funds is of portfolios of investments and not as much individual companies and therefore, like funds of funds, it is also rare for someone to move from a secondary to a PE fund.

- Firms that manage secondary funds include Lexington Partners; Landmark Partners; Coller Capital; Pomona Capital and Paul Capital.

Who Is Who At PE Funds

In addition to knowing the differences between fund types, it's vital that you become fluent in the different roles at PE and VC funds. As well as knowing the appropriate level at which to enter a fund, you should be able to distinguish between the different levels of professionals you are meeting. To sound informed you need to know what each of these people do and how they fit into the investment process. Below are some definitions we give for different titles. We believe these are the most commonly accepted titles, but they can refer to different professional levels depending on the fund (for example, some funds use Associate, Senior Associate, VP or even Principal for the role immediately out of business school). So, pay attention to specific funds' individual classifications.

ANALYST

- Pre-MBA
- Almost always the most junior professional at the fund
- Some are hired directly out of undergrad while others may have some initial work experience
- Those that are hired with more experience are still always pre-MBA and typically have three years or less of total work experience (these are most often from investment banking/consulting programs but could also include finance roles in accounting or industry, etc.)
- Generally works on basic deal support including research, analysis, financial modeling and valuation

- Hiring at this level is not common in the industry, however at more institutional/ mature funds Analysts can be brought on for two- to three-year programs that are similar to the investment banking and consulting training programs. After completing these programs, the Analysts may even move on to another fund as an Associate before going to business school

ASSOCIATE

- The title can be used at both the pre- and post-MBA level although the majority of firms classify it as pre-MBA
- This is the most common initial entry point into the various types of private equity funds
- Generally have five or less years of total work experience most frequently from a traditional investment banking or consulting program
- Usually the most junior professional at a fund (or second most junior at a fund with Analysts) and are typically hired out of the two- to three-year investment banking or consulting programs
- Associates have more interaction with senior professionals than Analysts and may oversee Analysts if the fund has them

SENIOR ASSOCIATE

- Have zero to two years of post-MBA or equivalent experience (very commonly hired directly out of business school)
- Typically not the most junior person, might even be the number two person on some deal teams
- Usually between four and seven years of total work experience
- Conduct due diligence on potential new investments and work to support the fund's portfolio companies
- Get involved beyond support to actual execution (begin to be involved in deal negotiations, etc.)
- Compensation usually includes a portion of carried interest

VICE PRESIDENT

- Usually have one to six years of post-MBA or equivalent work experience and usually six to nine years of total work experience
- Typically the number two person on deal teams
- Beginning to lead more senior execution tasks and some initial deal negotiations.
- Compensation almost always includes a portion of the carried interest

PRINCIPAL

- Have four to nine years of post-MBA or equivalent work experience and usually eight to 13 years of total work experience
- Typically run day-to-day deal process and manage a team of investment professionals
- Quarterback the majority of typical deal execution
- Position includes carried interest

PARTNER (includes General Partner, Managing Partner)

- Most senior professionals in the firm
- Generally have at least seven years experience post-MBA and often much more
- May be one of the founders or original Partners in the fund
- Responsible for managing their own deals. Also usually involved in fund management and operational issues including fundraising, hiring decisions and overall fund strategy
- Position includes a substantial portion of the carried interest

EMPLOYMENT TERMS

Throughout this book you will find references to the "traditional" career path and whether a candidate is "on-cycle" or "off-cycle." As we mentioned in the introduction, the traditional path for someone looking to become a long-term player in private equity is known as 2-2-2—two years in an investment banking or management consulting program after undergrad, two years in a private equity/LBO firm and then two years in business school. If all goes well, the next step after business school would be a full-time Partner-track position at a PE firm. Once again, this guide will address people who have followed or are currently immersed in that traditional path, but it will also take an in-depth look at those people who were able to get into private equity without following the 2-2-2 path.

"On-cycle" and "off-cycle" are terms used to describe the timing of pre- and current MBA hiring cycles. As we explain in Chapters IV and V, PE firms have been making offers to Analysts in investment banking and consulting programs and to business school students as early as the end of their first year. If a pre-MBA Analyst is interviewing during the summer or early fall between their first and second years for a position that begins in the following summer, he/she is considered on-cycle. A candidate who is interviewing for a position that starts before the natural end of their current commitment (usually July for Analyst programs) is said to be "off-cycle." "Off-cycle" can also refer to the timing of a firm that interviews for immediate hires (they are looking to pull someone out of their program early). Similarly, a firm that begins to interview as late as January-April would be considered "late-cycle" if they are looking for someone to start that same June or July.

chapter II

The Market Today

The private equity market has gone through a major transformation over the past two decades with much of the changes occurring over the past two years. The changes have had a dramatic impact on hiring. As you are likely aware, you are attempting to enter one of the highest profile sectors of the financial markets—one that is wielding significant influence on the economy while at the same time creating great wealth for its investors. The wealth that has been amassed has played a significant role in increasing the attractiveness of the sector and in making it an even more competitive environment to enter. This chapter will give a brief overview of the current private equity market, including how the market has matured into a global industry that is attracting new powerful investors. It will also touch on how the changes have affected career opportunities for different pools of candidates and how the surging hedge fund market is affecting hiring.

The PE market is stronger by many measures than it has ever been. Money continues to flow strongly into the market—in 2006 buyout funds raised a record $149 billion, 40% more than the previous mark set in 2005. 2006 was also a strong year for venture capital fundraising as VC firms brought in $25 billion in new funds, according to *Private Equity Analyst* data. At the same time new funds are being created, existing LPs are increasing their commitments and new ones are jumping on board. Funds that focused on the U.S. markets are now taking their investment expertise abroad and the LPs are following. Most industry pros expect PE funds will be able to consistently raise capital and to steadily produce strong risk-adjusted returns well into the future.

Today's PE market bears little resemblance to the market of 25 years ago. Private equity funds have grown from a cottage industry with a few practitioners to a major force in the financial world. As recently as November 2004, an article in *The Economist* titled, The New Kings of Capitalism, pointed out that, at the time, The Blackstone Group alone had equity stakes in about 40 portfolio companies, which, combined had over 300,000 employees and annual revenue of more than $50 billion. If they were a single unit, the holdings would have made Blackstone one of the top 20 Fortune 500 firms. Blackstone is not the only mega fund. The Economist article noted that Texas Pacific Group's portfolio companies had over 255,000 employees and revenue of $41 billion, while The Carlyle Group's portfolio companies had 150,000 employees and revenue of $31 billion. With their recent deals those firms are even bigger now.

CHART 3
Annual Buyout/Venture Capital Fundraising

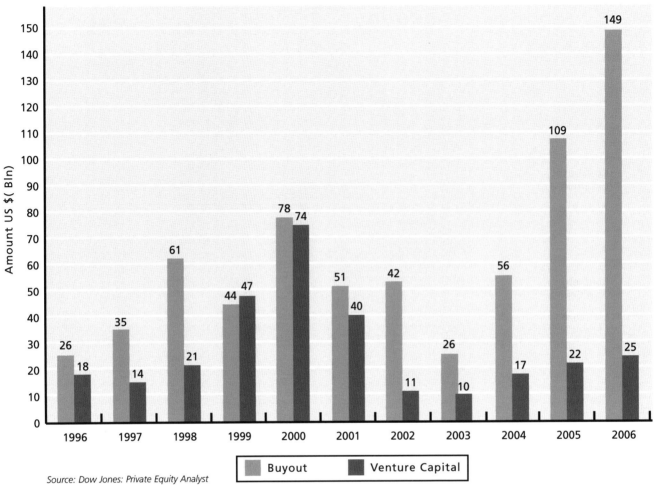

Source: Dow Jones: Private Equity Analyst

In 1980, Kohlberg Kravis Roberts & Co. ran the world's largest buyout fund at $135 million, according to *The Economist*. In today's buyout world, in which firms compete to one-up each other, $1 billion funds are commonplace and the $16 billion barrier has been broken. As this guide was going to press in early 2007, Kohlberg Kravis Roberts & Company and The Blackstone Group were getting ready to announce funds with more than $20 billion and Goldman Sachs was close to capping off its own $19 billion fund. Providence Equity Partners had announced that it had raised $12 billion for a media and communications fund—the largest specialized fund raised to date. Pools of capital are also becoming more sophisticated and PE firms are adding new asset classes to their stable of investment vehicles. In addition to its mega-LBO funds, Blackstone manages mezzanine, real estate and funds of funds. Carlyle runs leveraged finance, buyout, venture and growth capital and real estate funds. Although the large funds get a lot of attention, there are also still many small PE funds, and it is not uncommon to find one run by just a handful of investment professionals.

CHART 4
Ten Largest Closed PE-Backed LBOs *(as of 12/31/2006)*

Rank	Firm Name	Target	Value (in billions)	Year
1	Bain Capital/Kohlberg Kravis Roberts & Co./ Merrill Lynch Global Private Equity	HCA Inc.	$33.00	2006
2	Kohlberg Kravis Roberts & Co.	RJR Nabisco	$31.40	1989
3	Blackstone Group/Carlyle Group/ Permira/Texas Pacific Group	Freescale Semiconductor Inc.	$17.60	2006
4	Clayton Dubilier & Rice/The Carlyle Group/ Merrill Lynch Global Private Equity	Hertz Corp.	$15.00	2005
5	Cerberus Capital Management/ Citigroup/Aozora Bank	General Motors Acceptance Corp.	$14.00	2006
6	Apax Partners/Blackstone Group/ Kohlberg Kravis Roberts & Co./Permira/ Providence Equity Partners	TDC AS	$12.90	2006
7	Silver Lake Partners/Blackstong Group/ Texas Pacific Group/Thomas H. Lee Partners/ Kohlberg Kravis Roberts & Co./Goldman Sachs/ Bain Capital	SunGard Data Systems Inc.	$11.30	2005
8	Kohlberg Kravis Roberts & Co./Silver Lake Partners/ AlpInvest Partners/Apax Partners/Bain Capital	NXP semiconductor business of Royal Philips Electronics	$10.59	2006
9	Blackstone Group/Carlyle Group/ Kohlberg Kravis Roberts & Co.	VNU	$9.70	2006
10	Kohlberg Kravis Roberts & Co./ Five Mile Capital Partners/Goldman Sachs Capital Partners	GMAC Commercial Holding Corp.	$9.00	2006

Source: Buyouts

THE MARKET

Investments in PE funds continue to be driven by large institutions. Institutional backers including the California Public Employees' Retirement System (CalPERs), the Pennsylvania State Employees' Retirement System, the Canada Pension Plan Investment Board, the New York State Teachers' Retirement System, the Oregon Investment Council, and the Teachers' Retirement System of Illinois have been consistent investors in PE funds. Newcomers such as the New Jersey State Investment Council and the New Mexico Public Employees' Retirement Fund made recent investments.

Over the past several years the PE market has also grown into a global industry, both in terms of where funds are making investments and in the profile of the LPs. There are large global firms that oversee investments in many different countries. As private equity firms have looked for new investments, one region that has attracted significant interest is China where more than 300 firms have already opened offices. Bain Capital plans to establish a $1 billion fund focused on China. In fact, at $10 billion, Greater China which includes China, Hong Kong and Taiwan, was the second largest market for private equity in Asia in 2006 and accounted for 18% of all private equity investment sin Asia. Since 2000 the market had grown 74%.

CHART 5
Top 10 Most Active Venture Capital Investors of 2006

2006 Rank	2005 Rank	Firm Name	No. of Deals 2005	No. of Deals 2006
1	1	Draper Fisher Jurvetson (FKA: Draper Associates)	79	82
2	2	New Enterprise Associates	75	75
3	12	Intel Capital	46	75
4	7	Polaris Venture Partners	50	64
5	8	Kleiner Perkins Caufield & Byers	49	62
6	3	U.S. Venture Partners	69	60
7	21	Oak Investment Partners	38	56
8	6	Sequoia Capital	50	55
9	5	Venrock Associates	58	50
10	22	Austin Ventures, L.P.	38	47
11	36	Foundation Capital	31	45
12	28	Highland Capital Partners LLC	34	44
13	20	InterWest Partners	40	43
14	16	Village Ventures	42	43
15	17	Benchmark Capital	40	42

Source: Venture Capital Journal

In addition to the U.S.-based Limited Partners that have increased their investments in PE funds, as the industry has matured and prospered the asset class has been able to attract capital from global players, no doubt because they value the above average returns. GIC Special Investments, the private equity arm of the Government of Singapore Investment Corp., invested in KKR's first buyout fund in the 1980s and has been a steady investor in PE ever since. Dutch pension funds Pensioenfunds PGGM and ABP invest in the market via AlpInvest Partners and the National Pension Reserve Fund of Ireland is an investor in U.S. and European PE funds. At the same time, major LPs including CalPERs and the Washington State Investment Board for the first time put money to work in funds that invest in Asia.

The industry is also viewed in a better light today than it was a few decades ago. In fact, the buyout industry counts among its ranks well-known business leaders, celebrities and former politicians including Jack Welch (Clayton, Dubilier & Rice), Lou Gerstner and Arthur Levitt (Carlyle), the U2 rocker Bono (Elevation Partners) and former U.S. Treasury Secretary Paul O'Neill (Blackstone). On the VC side, Colin Powell is a Strategic Limited Partner at Kleiner Perkins Caufield & Byers.

The Employment Scene:
A Competitive, But Improved Market

It's not surprising that as the size and scope of PE funds has changed over the years, so too have their hiring habits. There are more firms hiring than ever before and in a given year many bring on multiple new people. That means, of course, that the demand for highly capable people is as strong as it has ever been.

THE MARKET

CHART 6
Evolution of the Buyout Market

	1994	2006
No. of LBO Firms in Existence	347	593
No. of LBO Funds in Existence	512	1,040
No. of Professionals	3,706	9,057
No. of First Time LBO Funds Raised	27	38
No. of LBO Funds Raising Money	110	179
LBO Capital Under Management ($B)	113.6	636.5
Avg LBO Capital Under Mgt per Firm ($M)	327.4	1,073.3
Avg LBO Fund Size to Date ($M)	199.7	442.7
Avg LBO Fund Size Raised ($M)	247.7	1,114.8

Source: Thomson Financial/NVCA

As recruiters, we break down the hiring market in terms of supply and demand—the supply of people looking for jobs vs. the demand from firms looking to hire. Although in PE the demand never really exceeds the supply (meaning there are always more qualified people looking for jobs than there are positions available), on a relative basis the situation has improved in favor of job seekers, particularly for pre-MBAs finishing their investment banking and consulting programs and graduating MBAs. A lot of the improvement is due to the spectacular fundraising in 2005 and 2006, which has led to the need for more investment professionals to put that money to work (we go into more detail about pre-MBA and MBA hiring in Chapters IV and V).

Looking at how the PE market has evolved over the last 10 years gives additional clues about the hiring market. As we have discussed, the industry has grown. Indeed, Chart 6 shows the amount of capital under management has more than quadrupled, the number of professionals working in the industry has nearly doubled and thus the amount of capital-per-professional has increased over time. The initial conclusion we can draw is that the industry is most likely not overstaffed. Larger funds have been raised and deal sizes have increased, but our observation is that PE funds have maintained disciplined hiring.

The Hedge Fund Effect

As of the end of the 2006 there were approximately $1.4 trillion in assets under management in the hedge fund industry, well above the $637 billion in buyout funds and the $268 billion in venture capital, according to Thomson Financial/NVCA data. The surging hedge fund market has grown into an asset class that increasingly competes with PE funds for top talent. Hedge funds will often hire candidates who have multiple PE offers or take candidates out of investment banking programs early. There have been two measurable consequences of this competition from hedge funds—a few more available positions for PE job seekers (as long as hedge funds keep growing, some candidates who consider both PE and hedge fund jobs, will take the hedge fund offer leaving more seats open to those people dedicated to landing a PE job) and an increase in compensation (see Chapter XII for a more in-depth discussion on compensation). However, if the hedge fund market crashes, the private equity job market will have a larger pool of candidates to choose from and may not have to pay up as much as they have been to attract top talent.

chapter III

Out Of Undergrad

Like many college students, you may be beginning to think about your career after school. If you have a passion for investing and are attracted by the allure of owning businesses and influencing their strategies you may be considering the private equity industry as a long-term career. You likely have questions about how to break into PE and what the optimal path is.

When hiring at the pre-MBA level (note: this term doesn't mean that all candidates hired at this level eventually attend business school), most PE funds focus exclusively on candidates in Analyst programs at investment banks and consulting firms. These candidates bring a level of deal experience, financial skills and maturity that someone right out of college does not. If you ask private equity veterans whether you should pursue a job with a PE fund directly out of undergrad, they would most likely recommend against it and we would agree. While there are a small number of quality PE funds that do hire at this level, the vast majority don't, so, in our opinion, spending too much time pursuing those jobs may be a losing battle and a big distraction. As someone still in college, the best way to pursue a PE career is to get on the right path to secure an Analyst position in investment banking or consulting. Trying to take a different track can sometimes backfire later in life (see Chapter V for Case Studies of people who struggled to enter PE after following a non-traditional path earlier). Now is the time in which you are ideally positioned to take the best first step.

The Traditional Path

Although we will introduce you to someone who bucked the trend by landing a PE job straight from undergrad (Case Study 7 in Chapter IV), he is an exception. The bulk of our advice to undergrads focuses on the merits of following the traditional path. The traditional path to a career in PE usually commences in a quality structured two- to three-year investment banking or management consulting program. These programs are the PE world's version of field training in which Analysts get extensive deal and/or project exposure that will provide the foundation for working in PE. Most funds view both types of programs as part of the hands on training needed to make the transition from college into the coveted PE job (think of this as PE's answer to the residency program that doctors must go through). Additionally, the banking/consulting job will leave you with contacts that will be invaluable to your long-term career.

The choices you make coming out of college will affect your future ability to get into private equity. You should think about whether you have what it takes to get into an elite training program at a bulge-bracket bank. If you don't, maybe you should target a middle-market firm. Both firm types have merits. It's up to you to choose which is best for you. As you will read later, many larger PE funds look to recruit the best Analysts from top programs and some funds will target banks even more specifically by the deals on which they focus (i.e., large- vs. middle-market).

Positioning Yourself For An Analyst Program

Getting into a renowned banking/consulting program is like going to a university with a powerhouse Division I sports program: it will give you the most visibility to be drafted by a professional team, or in this case a top-flight PE fund. We estimate about 2,000-2,500 undergrads are hired each year into mid to large investment banking and consulting programs in the U.S. All the bulge-bracket investment banks have Analyst training programs as do most of the regional and middle-market banks and the major consulting firms. Our research shows that in 2006 the leading investment banks, including Bear Stearns, Citigroup, Credit Suisse, Goldman Sachs, JPMorgan Chase, Lehman Brothers, Merrill Lynch and Morgan Stanley, combined brought in about 900 first-year Analysts in their North American offices. On the consulting side firms including Bain & Company, Boston Consulting Group, McKinsey & Company and the Monitor Group had about 400 first-year Analysts on their payrolls.

Securing a spot in one of these Analyst programs may not be easy, especially if those banks and/or consulting firms do not recruit on your campus, but there are steps you can take to improve your chances of receiving an offer. Perhaps the most useful is to focus on getting a formal banking/consulting internship during the summer after your junior year of college. As we pointed out in the introduction to this guide, committing early to a PE career is essential. The same is true when looking for a summer internship. If you are a sophomore, this is the best time to begin planning your path.

UNDERGRAD

For the few fortunate ones, the right summer experience between your sophomore and junior years will give you a leg up to secure the coveted investment-banking/consulting internship before your senior year, which in turn will help you get into an Analyst program at an investment bank or consulting firm when you graduate. For others it will be getting whatever structured finance or accounting exposure you can.

Glocap Insight

Think of a summer banking/consulting internship in the same way a baseball player would view going to a summer baseball camp to improve his chances of playing at a major university. Just as the ballplayer will learn new skills, fine-tune existing ones and meet coaches with connections, so too will the banking/consulting internship help you hone your talents and meet people that can help you along the way.

Your friends may be off to the beach, but for you, getting the most out of your summer will be the first step to differentiating yourself and demonstrating your commitment to a PE career. While these summer jobs are not necessary requirements, they are extremely helpful and banking/consulting programs look favorably on those who have used their summers wisely. If you are a senior and did not use the summer to your advantage you may have to play catch up by widening your search of investment banks or non-bank alternatives that will accept you.

Assuming you land an Analyst position after college, if at any point you have a choice of where to work, you should choose a group that will give you the skills most translatable to PE funds. The groups within an investment bank that most closely meet those criteria are the leveraged finance/high-yield, private equity (not private placements), financial sponsors or M&A groups. Some industry groups within investment banks integrate those functions. PE funds that have an industry focus such as media or healthcare will find additional value in candidates who have worked in those specific groups. Some well-known consulting firms have PE, corporate finance or valuation groups that teach some of the same skills.

Other Options

If you don't get into an investment banking or consulting Analyst training program all hope is not lost. Accounting firms have transaction and valuation groups that also involve heavy financial modeling and can be a good lead-in to PE (see Case Study 6). Also, doing internal corporate M&A at a major corporation (such as GE or Microsoft) can sometimes provide many similar skills.

What If I'm Offered A PE Job Straight After Graduation?

Although there are PE funds that will give someone out of college a shot, in our view there are only a handful that are very high-quality places. To us, those are the ones with a training program, where you are entering with a class of Analysts and where you will be exposed to different investment stages. If you find such a fund and get an offer it may be worth taking as it could potentially put you on a faster track to a long-term career in PE. Having said that, since very few large, quality, stand-alone funds hire out of undergrad, you should question whether the opportunities that may be available to you directly out of college are the ones that you should be pursuing to best prepare for a long-term career in PE.

If you end up at a fund which, by its nature, offers less structured training compared to that offered by investment banks and consulting firms you could very likely only focus on closing one or two deals (or even none!) during your first couple of years there so learning could be spotty. You could also join a PE/LBO fund and be focused on doing mainly research and prospecting for deals over the phone. Although those are valued skills for some growth equity funds where they can lead to successful career paths, they are not as applicable across all types of funds and do not always replace hands-on deal execution experience. If you get an offer from a fund that is not a well-known name we would advise that you proceed with caution. Working at such a fund may not allow you to build the platform of necessary skills and make the contacts that you will need if you want to build a long-term career in private equity. If you feel like you have a golden opportunity you should at least ask what you will be doing at that fund because, depending on your role (like a predominantly cold calling one that the person in Case Study 7 got), you may or may not get what you want out of the experience which should be to best position yourself for the longer term PE career you want to work toward.

Glocap Insight

Taking a job at a less-structured PE fund straight out of undergrad can have a similar downside to being home schooled—you may have smart "parents" and you will learn a lot, but you will be missing out on the classroom environment and the interaction with your peers.

UNDERGRAD

chapter IV

From An Analyst Program

If you're currently in an investment banking or consulting program and think you're on the right path to a job in private equity, you may still need a reality check. If there is anything more you could be doing to better position yourself, you want to know what it is.

Everything is going according to plan. You're entrenched in step one of the traditional 2-2-2 path and are heading toward step two. Nevertheless, now is not the time to take anything for granted. To show you what you are up against, let's go over some numbers. As we stated in Chapter III, there about 2,000-2,500 undergrads hired each year into mid to large investment-banking and consulting programs in the U.S. Whereas 10 years ago there might have been 10-20 PE funds that consistently hired at the pre-MBA level, we now estimate that there are over 250 firms that bring in a total of 300-400 pre-MBA Analysts (again, even though we call them pre-MBA, not all go on to business school). This means there is demand for only about 15% of the Analysts in investment banking and consulting programs. It goes without saying, that those who make the cut will be the best of the best.

With that in mind, your course of action at this point should not be dissimilar from the process of applying to Analyst programs described in the previous chapter. You will have to prove yourself once again. Just as the undergrad process began as far back as your sophomore year, you must plan early if you want to successfully move on to the next phase of your career. The Case Studies in this section emphasize the importance of getting an early start. In addition to those stories, we also recommend you read Case Studies 10-12 from MBAs in Chapter V as those people went through the pre-MBA process as well and offer useful insight into how they succeeded.

One point worth mentioning is that whatever private equity job you do get at this point will not necessarily be a long-term position. PE funds hire junior professionals as Analysts or Associates in support roles and expect them to work hard and contribute, but, except for a small percentage of funds, most do not leave much room for a long-term commitment. The large majority of PE funds brings junior professionals on for two to three years, but then hold fast to the idea that they must move on—potentially to business school or another opportunity. However, some funds from this group make exceptions and allow those Analysts or Associates who they believe will be true stars to remain with the fund instead of going to business school. Finally, there is an even smaller group of funds that are open from day one to having junior professionals stay on and move up within the firm.

We cannot emphasize enough that PE firms want superior individuals who are mature, driven, hard working and possess top analytical skills. PE funds are not in the business of teaching you how to construct a discounted cash flow or LBO model. Not only do they expect you to be able to put together a model, they want you to be able to flawlessly analyze complex and challenging deals and use your business judgment to develop conclusions about the analysis. Additionally, they require effective and polished communications skills. No matter where you are now, it should go without saying that you should be striving to rise to the top of your Analyst class because most funds want the A+ Analysts.

The Race For The Best

PE funds compete each year for the top pre-MBA talent. If you're one of these elite Analysts you usually know it—you're probably in a top group at a top firm; you've been invited to work on live deals with extensive modeling, have traveled for the firm and received a positive mid-year review. Over the last few years the competition for the leading Analysts has picked up in intensity due to the tight market and the record amount of capital that has flowed into the industry (see Chart 3, Chapter II). The demand has become so great that a lot of funds (especially larger ones that make multiple hires for each Analyst class) are starting their searches earlier each year to ensure they are previewing all of the best Analysts before they are hired by other funds or commit to staying on longer at their current firms. Some PE funds even extend offers for positions a full year in advance (see Case Study 1 for the story of an on-cycle hire). The accelerated hiring has been led by the mega funds and there has been a trickle down effect on hiring at all funds that want to get the best talent available. For example, under the new pace, funds that used to make offers to Analysts in February of their last year are now hiring in November and the ones that hired in October are hiring in July or August or earlier.

> ### Glocap Insight
>
> We estimate that approximately 80% of the Analysts in investment banks and consulting firms who receive offers from PE funds will have them by the 18-month mark of their Analyst programs, although this percentage has increased in each of the last several years.

If you are fortunate enough to be a top Analyst from a renowned program the opportunities will come your way and you should be able to choose where you want to work. But, to be ready for the onslaught of PE firms and recruiters who will approach you, you must begin your preparations in the first six months of your training program. That means getting your resume together early into your first year. You should also start to familiarize yourself with the different types of PE funds—what they do and how you might fit in. It may sound early, but that is how competitive it has become. Your decision on which fund to join will be based on which is the best fit for you (see *Evaluating Your Choices*, Chapter IX).

Opportunities For Others

Each year there are hundreds of other qualified Analysts who complete investment-banking and consulting training programs at bulge bracket and boutique firms across the country. The process of getting into a private equity fund out of an Analyst training program is like a professional sports draft. In this case it is funds that go after the same top Analyst talent. But, we have found that once those Analysts match-up, accept offers and are out of the market (which is usually by the end of the summer), the PE firms then sit down with their internal teams and recruiters and review how many openings they still have and begin looking at the people who were not initially considered—including those who may not have been in the market yet. PE funds know that there will be future stars in that group of candidates as well. As mentioned, for the firms that hire early it's a mad dash to get to the top performing, top pedigree candidates from the premier investment banks, but not all the funds fill their staffing needs from that pool or necessarily rely on it exclusively. There is generally a predictable second wave of recruiting that occurs and, that is most likely where you come in. From our experience, there are Analysts who get jobs later in the cycle (see Case Study 4) and then can move up and shine as bright as anyone else.

Our first recommendation therefore would be to be patient. Unlike the larger funds that know in advance how many junior professionals they need, there are other funds that may not know their hiring needs until closer to the end of your Analyst program (meaning they are hiring later in the cycle). If you are a top performer from a regional or middle-market bank slots should be available for you. From our experience, there are always some hiring firms that say, "I need someone who can crunch numbers and think on their feet—a great raw 'deal' athlete. I'm indifferent as to which school or firm they come from." Given the choice between a B+ candidate from a bulge-bracket banking program and an A+ candidate from a boutique investment bank, the fund will often take the A+ person, many times referred to in the industry as the "better athlete" (see Case Study 4).

In all, you've got to be realistic. If you know certain exclusive firms are less likely to pursue you, focus instead on the ones that will be more interested in your middle-market or boutique background. These can include some larger funds, but probably more middle-market and/or regional ones. Recruiters may still call you for these positions, but not as early in the cycle. That doesn't mean you should not reach as high as you want and start as early as you can. The strategy is similar to when you were a senior in high school and you divided the colleges you were applying to into "reach" schools and "safety" schools. You should do the same with PE funds—have your "reach" funds, but have your "safer" funds as well and target them specifically.

We have found that some funds are absolutely open to hiring Analysts from middle-market and regional investment banks and, in some cases, may even prefer to do so over a bulge-bracket banker. Take the example of a $300 million fund based outside of a major city that concentrates its investments in smaller companies in the same geography. More often than not these types of funds can be targeting closely held or even family businesses and will look for a person who understands businesses of this size and can relate to the local culture of the targeted investment companies.

Insider Tip

PE INVESTMENT PROFESSIONAL

"I would say, don't even think of working at a private equity firm unless you can think on your feet and can make decisions with sometimes limited input."

"To me, the most important attributes/skills of a private equity Analyst/Associate are: ability to quickly understand what drives a business; strong analytical capability (beyond quantitative skills); and being able to think and act outside a structured environment (outside the box)."

"I felt I was best prepared for my career in private equity because of my love for math and engineering, and having worked in various businesses beginning at a young age. To me, it is very important that a candidate "fit" in with the personality of my firm. When hiring someone I also take into consideration the reason why they want to do it. If it is to prove something or for the money, then they are wrong candidates. Someone who feels passionate will almost always succeed."

Even though the path you will follow differs from that of bulge-bracket Analysts, you must understand (and work within) the same hiring cycle as they did. If the job search of a bulge-bracket Analyst is a sprint, yours is more of a marathon pace that can stretch from September to January or beyond. However, you too should get your resume ready early and pace yourself. You may have to work harder and be more creative and will have to be more convincing about why PE is for you. You will be grilled harder and scrutinized

more in interviews by Partners who wonder if you can help them and their investors make money. The Partners will examine you to see if you are who they want representing their firm at the highest level.

What About Consultants?

While there has historically been a preference for PE candidates with investment banking training, there are some firms that consistently hire consultants and the trend has been growing steadily. PE funds have been trying different methods to get more value out of their investments. This includes improving the operations of the companies in which they invest and paying more attention to their overall business strategy. Both of those play more to the training of consultants than that of bankers. More specifically, we have noticed recently that more funds that used to fill four pre-MBA positions with investment banking Analysts are now bringing on three bankers and one consultant to balance the hardcore financial analytics with some strategy/operations training. There are even a handful of funds that have expressed a strong *preference* to only hire consultants and a smaller group that, as a rule, *exclusively* hire consultants over bankers. Alumni from consulting firms probably make up 10-20% of the PE industry, so it is no surprise that firms with former consultants value that training and skill set. If you are coming out of a consulting program it could make the most sense to first target those firms.

CASE STUDIES

Following are some Case Studies involving pre-MBA Analysts. The first five are from candidates who got into their PE funds the traditional way—out of banking/consulting programs. We also have an example of someone who got a pre-MBA position with an accounting background. And, finally we also include the stories of three exceptions—one person who got in directly out of undergrad and two who benefitted from specialized technology and healthcare industry experience. All of these candidates had stellar professional backgrounds and records of strong academic achievement. Whether they were "first round draft picks" or a later selection, the authors of the Case Studies paint a good picture of how they conducted their job searches while at the same time maintaining their day jobs and working long hours. You too will also have to squeeze in phone interviews and day trips to different cities for face-to-face interviews (Chapter XI goes over what to do once you get an interview). The bulge-bracket Analysts may find that their firms are more accommodating (especially if it is during the real sprint times described earlier) as getting hired is a good reflection on them. Others may have to deal with banks and consulting firms that are less accommodating, making the search that much more taxing. Either way, it was a grind for these people and could be for you as well. Pay careful attention to the advice each person gives and how they describe their interviews and their job search process. The resumes that correspond to some of these Case Studies and others that appear later in the book can be found in Chapter X.

CASE STUDY 1
Bulge-Bracket On Cycle Hire
(see Resume 1)

This person went from an Analyst training program at a bulge bracket investment bank to a buyout shop. It is an example of an on-cycle candidate who went through more of a summer sprint. He knew early on that he wanted private equity, excelled at all levels and landed a top job.

"I started looking into getting a job in private equity well before the end of my first year of Analyst training. I had my resume ready by mid-July because I had heard from people in prior years that the hiring market would heat up by the end of the summer. Unfortunately, I got a bit crushed at work and my search didn't really take hold until late August (although I was contacted by a recruiter in July) when I got my resume out. I interviewed at five firms during a three-week stretch beginning in mid-September. I went to the first round at two places, the second round at two other places and into a fifth round at the firm that eventually extended me an offer.

> *"Of course, I'd recommend others start as early as possible for the sheer value of not missing out on an interview at a place you'd be interested in."*

When I graduated from undergrad in 2004 with a degree in economics I was not thinking private equity. My thoughts going into the Analyst program were that I would do as well as I could, hopefully enjoy it and maybe make a career out of it. I didn't want to look past it. I was randomly placed in the natural resources group at my bank which was good and bad—good because with oil prices soaring there were a ton of deals and I was working on non-stop live deals from the beginning, bad because I was absolutely overwhelmed by the work load. I liked what I was doing but knew I would need a change. I had pitched some deals to PE funds and also talked with a lot of friends and other Analysts as the year went on about the merits of working in PE.

I definitely feel lucky that I started when I did and found a job so early into the process. Having an offer early into my second year has made things a lot more relaxed for me. I can see the light at the end of the tunnel.

I would advise other banking Analysts interested in PE to be sure they want this career well before the recruiting period comes up. You've got to go after it hard so you better want it and do your homework, especially when it comes to preparing for interviews. It sounds obvious to say that you better know your LBO models and your deals inside and out, but it's true. On my interviews I was grilled pretty hard by the Partners. The firm that eventually extended me an offer had me meet just about everyone that I would be working with, that meant about 12-15 people. About half of them asked me about my work and the others just wanted to get to know me and see if I would fit in with the firm. All the other firms asked me pretty technical questions. They asked me to walk them through an LBO model. Some would show me an LBO model and say, 'Let's say the depreciation changes by $1 million, talk about how every line in your model changes.'

Of course, I'd recommend others start as early as possible for the sheer value of not missing out on an interview at a place you'd be interested in. Personally, I wasn't interested in working at a large shop like a KKR or a Blackstone. I've heard they're the ones that are pushing the process earlier and earlier as they go after the number one guys in the leveraged finance groups. I knew I wanted a smaller, more collegial shop and didn't target a specific style of investing. The firm I ended up with was in the market for three people and I was the first they hired."

CASE STUDY 2
Bulge-Bracket Banker—With A Late Start

This person grew up knowing about private equity and achieved a successful transition into PE by going to a top banking program.

"Growing up in Silicon Valley, I was exposed to the venture capital world early on. I knew I wanted to go into VC and began moving in that direction as a senior in college, when I focused on getting into a banking program. I knew the program would be a great experience and give me skills in finance and be a good launching pad for me. I came out of undergrad with a degree in business administration. I also knew I wanted to join the tech group of whichever Analyst program I went to. I took advantage of the on campus interviews, was offered a spot in a top banking program and accepted. Since I was allowed to state my preferred industry, I listed technology.

I was first approached by headhunters and some PE funds that don't use headhunters just after I finished the first year of my Analyst program. The funds try to get you to commit before you get offered, and possibly accept, a position as a third-year Analyst. I wasn't looking to get into buyouts as I was still interested in VC, but had to be realistic. There were simply less venture opportunities out there. I ended up interviewing at a buyout/growth equity shop.

My first interview wasn't until late November or early December of my second year. A headhunter pointed me to the fund and someone from my bank also had a contact at the firm. I interviewed with five firms and for me the process went very fast. I was already in the process with other funds when this one contacted me. I think the banking program really gave me the skills and industry knowledge that opened a lot of doors for me in the world of private equity. Many funds like to hire ex-bankers, but a good number of people hired come from consulting or other backgrounds, as long as they have the necessary skills and experience.

> "Even though I knew that some PE funds were beginning the hiring process very early, I wasn't concerned that I didn't have an offer until well into my second year."

The entire search process was pretty grueling and time consuming as you have to do your day job at the same time as you are managing your search. Luckily, my bank was very supportive (as I suspect are others). They know how the process works and were good about letting me go on interviews. The toughest part was trying to figure out what you want to do and differentiating between firms because there are so many of them. I'd advise candidates to do their homework. I wouldn't have been able to see all of what is out there without a recruiter. I would also advise people to leverage their networks and not to be afraid to ask senior people at their banks for help.

If I could do it all over, one additional thing I would have done is to try to explore more. There are so many funds out there you want to make sure you are focusing on the ones where you will enjoy working. Sometimes you are in the middle of your search and then a fund gives you an offer and they want a quick answer. There is no time to delay. Even though I knew that some PE funds were beginning the hiring process very early, I wasn't concerned that I didn't have an offer until well into my second year. It was the big shops that have a strict recruiting schedule and were extending offers by Labor Day. I wasn't interested in going to one of those places. I knew they work you hard and I had done that in my banking program. I was looking for a better work/life balance. And, there were still plenty of jobs coming through."

CASE STUDY 3
Getting In From A Consulting Program
(see Resume 2)

Here is another person who didn't focus on PE early, but who leveraged consulting and industry experience.

"After graduating with a degree in engineering and a summer banking internship at a leading Wall Street bank, I co-founded a software company where I worked for 1? years. I subsequently returned to university to pursue a Masters degree in engineering. Upon receiving my Masters in 2002, I considered opportunities in industry, banking and consulting. I had not really even thought about private equity and did not have a great sense for what it was all about. I joined a top-tier consulting firm and worked hard developing my skills around market analysis and corporate strategy. During my time there, I had the opportunity to lead a tech and telecom project team. I had no master plan of working in private equity, but began to look for various opportunities at the beginning of my second year as a consultant. I considered a wide variety of options, including venture capital, industry and private equity. In each of these positions, I would be able to leverage my background in technology and strategy to be a value-added member of the team. For me, the decision to move into PE was more of an evolution of the things I had done. It was helpful during the process to talk with friends of mine who also worked in each of these respective industries.

> *"I would advise those looking for a job in PE to know your strengths and weaknesses and figure out where you are positioned well. Know the culture of the funds and come across as an engaging person. Go into interviews with confidence and determination."*

In my search, I didn't target big, late-stage buyout funds. Instead, I focused more on technology as an industry and sought out opportunities in that vertical. My approach was to take advantage of my technology and strategy background. I realized that I lacked formal finance training, so I didn't look too deeply into generalist firms where I had no advantage. Moreover, I was a little late to the game. While some people started in August or September, I didn't begin until late September or early October. My consulting job kept me on the road four days each week. And, while my firm was understanding, the process of working and searching for a job was grueling. As a backup, I also considered staying on with my firm for a third year. Eventually, I landed a job with a technology focused private equity fund that valued my consulting and technology experience.

For me, consulting prepared me very well for private equity. Bankers come into private equity with more muscles in finance, but consultants know competitive dynamics of particular industries. I also benefited from a track record of doing good work—in school and at my various jobs subsequent. Additionally, the graduate work that I had done in engineering helped to differentiate me from other candidates.

I would advise those looking for a job in PE to know your strengths and weaknesses and figure out where you are positioned well. Know the culture of the funds and come across as an engaging person. Go into interviews with confidence and determination. Show them that you know WHY you want to be in private equity and, more specifically, WHY you want to work for them. These are all extremely small organizations where every person is an important member of the team. It's similar to an athletic team with only a handful of members—come draft day, they want to know that you will be a good draft pick for them."

Getting In From A Regional Bank
(see Resume 3)

This is an example of someone who got into PE from a non-bulge-bracket bank and who secured a job late in the hiring cycle, proving that PE funds do come back for top candidates. Note how this person says being later in the cycle was actually a benefit.

"I did little during my undergrad years to prepare for a career in private equity. I got out of college in 2002 with an Ivy League degree in American History and didn't know what I wanted to do. I played baseball in college and was drawn to consulting and investment-banking because some of my past teammates had gone that route. Unfortunately, I had two hurdles in my way—my timing and my major. I began looking for my post-undergrad job in the fall of 2001, a time when the job market was tough and not many companies were visiting college campuses. With a major in American History I had no economics, no math and no finance.

I was able to interview with some of the New York banks (some of my interviews were pretty embarrassing as I had no idea what some of the basics, like EBITDA, were) but ended up getting an offer and taking it with a more regional bank in a smaller city. I think I was one of the last people they hired and fortunately they saw potential in me.

I had no clue what leveraged finance was, but that was where I was placed and it turned out to be a stroke of luck. My first 6-9 months were pretty painful getting up to speed on leveraged finance—I had never learned Excel or Powerpoint and that is what I lived and breathed. Looking back, it was good that I was in a small city. I had no problem working late into the night: there were no distractions and I had no school buddies around tugging at me.

I was accepted for a third year, but in the spring of my second year I started looking around and targeted private equity. Banking was getting routine. At a small firm there were only three people on each deal team so I got great deal experience. I knew there were a lot of bright and motivated people in private equity and liked the life/work balance. I knew I was not on cycle so I focused my search on 3-5 firms and used geography as a guide, staying away from larger cities. For me, headhunters were critical. My firm didn't focus much on helping me find a job. The headhunters got me the first contacts and got me in the door.

I ended up at a late-stage buy-out shop with several billion dollars under investment. I believe the two main reasons why I was considered at this firm were 1) my leveraged finance background (model-intensive and credit-focused) and 2) my deal experience (closing several transactions with M&A components). I don't think I was treated any differently in my interviews because of where I did my training—once you're in the room everyone focuses on your modeling skills, deal experience, critical thinking ability, and your personality.

I think two things helped me get into PE: I was coming out of leveraged finance, which is very model-intensive and credit-oriented. And, I was off cycle so I wasn't competing against every single Goldman and Blackstone second-year. I didn't look during my first year because I didn't know what I wanted and I wasn't that good. I was probably average during my first year (it took me nine months to learn Excel). By my second year, I was at the top of my class and felt I was in a position to look. I knew where I stood vis-à-vis the Analysts from the higher profile banking programs and I didn't feel like I was overlooked by the PE firms. I saw it more as I had job security with the third year offer (I made sure to put that on my resume). Being in a smaller city hurt me during the search process as I couldn't just hop over to see someone during lunch as people can in larger cities where the funds are concentrated. I was limited to phone interviews at first. Being off cycle benefited me in another way because later in the cycle the hiring firms seem to make quicker decisions. For me the entire process from first interview to final offer lasted about four weeks.

My job search became a type of second job and a secret life. It's a skill to balance your current obligations and not be able to talk about it with most people due to confidentiality. It is always stressful to interview and have your life on review, but I found that the more practice I got through phone interviews and with firms that I was less excited about the more my 'story' was honed and sharpened. I became comfortable speaking and talking about myself. Yes, there may be times when you'll need to get on a flight on short notice, but if you're paying yourself, usually you'll have about two weeks notice. The toughest part is juggling your current job responsibilities and traveling. I'd recommend talking and entrusting your job search with an Associate or VP who you feel comfortable with so they can give you advice and cover for you when you'll need it.

"Overall, I found that interviewers usually look highly on people who have been successful at each level of their life—high school, college, extra-curriculars, first job, etc. But in terms of doing anything differently or recommending my way, it's a tough call. I would guess the 'hit rate' for NYC banks is much higher for PE, vs. a regional bank. The key is to learn as much as you can where you are, and grab for responsibility."

Although my path was unique in the sense that I did not get into PE through a NYC i-bank, I think everyone's path is somewhat different from others. You may hit the perfect time in a recruiting cycle where they need a consultant-type person, or you may interview with a former athlete who understands the discipline and is impressed with your balance of school and sports in college, for example. Overall, I found that interviewers usually look highly on people who have been successful at each level of their life—high school, college, extra-curriculars, first job, etc. But in terms of doing anything differently or recommending my way, it's a tough call. I would guess the 'hit rate' for NYC banks is much higher for PE, vs. a regional bank. The key is to learn as much as you can where you are, and grab for responsibility.

My advice to pre-MBA candidates would be to put together a one page cheat sheet of your deals so you are ready for interviews. It should have revenue and EBITDA figures as well as any multiples and key factors that you can talk about. A lot of interviews honed in on deals so you should know the deal terms. I would also say, in addition to doing well in college, shining at your first job is critical. All firms are definitely looking for the top guys, no matter where they did their training.

I also did a lot of interviews with smaller firms for practice. I even did this with a few hedge funds and funds of funds. When they ask you 'Why do you want to go into private equity?' you better have an answer ready. Basically, all the interviews ask the same questions: Why do you want to go into private equity? Walk me through a deal you did? What was your role? If you were an investor would you have made this investment? Why? What was the industry landscape like? You should have answers ready for all of these questions."

CASE STUDY 5
Getting In From A Mid-Market Bank—Late Cycle
(see Resume 4)

The experiences of this candidate are a good example of how an Analyst at a mid-market bank can find a position. Although his interviews began later in the hiring cycle he didn't let that deter him.

"I had four internships in college. I worked with a stock-broker, at a venture capital firm, at a fledgling private equity fund and at a hedge fund. While I knew that I wanted to be in private equity after my internship experience, my mentor advised me that the best private equity players had investment banking experience, and that I should do the same before proceeding onwards. Thus, I began recruiting to get into investment banking with the full knowledge that I would be moving on after a few years. When I applied for the bulge bracket investment banking Analyst training programs neither my GPA nor my internships mattered. The banks clearly looked down on the school I attended and a perceived shortfall in formal business training. In addition, I wanted to stay close to home, which was not New York City, so there were limited options. Thus, without a bulge bracket extending its hand my way, I wound up taking a job at a mid-market investment bank. I rose to the top of my Analyst class. But, in my experience that is still a bit of an empty achievement in the eyes of the conservative private equity market and you don't get the respect you would if you had worked at a bulge bracket. It's a simple fact of life.

To move into private equity, I would have to work hard to dispel the thought that a bulge bracket investment banker is more valuable than a mid-market banker. I received a lot of flack for not coming out of the bulge-bracket program. I think the first question that came from most interviewers centered around, "With your board scores, GPA, and internship experience, why were you not at a bulge-bracket?" My response was the general "because I wanted to focus on smaller deals, work with a smaller deal team, and get some hands-on experience and not get lost at the bureaucracy of a bulge bracket." As I interview people, I now realize what nonsense that is. Every kid who is in a mid-market shop either had not gotten an offer from a bulge bracket, or took the mid-market job for other reasons.

What I had was experience at a private equity shop, deal experience, work ethic, and the knowledge of what I wanted. The realization that some of the industry's best bankers had moved on to become wildly successful in private equity, coupled with my affinity for the industry, decent pay and more reasonable hours, helped solidify my resolve to enter the market. My only questions revolved around how to market myself in an industry that typically caters to Analysts at bulge bracket investment banks.

"All in all, I think that as a middle-market banker, you have much more to offer than you may realize; you just need to identify those traits that set you apart and capitalize upon them."

In my Analyst program, I was able to work with smaller deal teams than those typically seen at the bureaucratic bulge brackets, which is an advantage with a lot of private equity shops that don't necessarily have an established hierarchy. While in investment banking, I reported directly to a Managing Director or Vice President. Today, I report directly to a Senior Managing Director. Having real deal experience on complex transactions, which many middle-market transactions certainly are, while still remaining relatively autonomous and resourceful is truly an asset and a great point to bring up to private equity shops.

Furthermore, I'd venture to say that a lot of the deals that will be lucrative for PE shops going forward will be proprietary or with companies that don't get widely auctioned. These companies are generally smaller and within the middle-market. The more experience you have executing deals for these companies, the better a resource you will be for a private equity fund. All in all, I think that as a middle-market banker, you have much more to offer than you may realize; you just need to identify those traits that set you apart and capitalize upon them.

I had gotten headhunter calls given that I was the top Analyst, but never really followed up on them. Since I was closely tied to the financial sponsor coverage effort, I knew a bit about which firms I'd like to explore further. An ex-Vice President at my firm helped secure a few interviews and from there I used a recruiter and specifically defined the types of shops that I wanted to eventually join. Between these two resources, I'd gotten five interviews; I flopped the first two, and, once I got comfortable interviewing, secured final rounds at two shops. One ultimately turned out to be the right fit and the opportunity I was really looking for. I started my search in March 2005 and finished by mid-April 2005, to eventually join the fund at the beginning of June 2005. That was a bit early, but I wanted to get a sense of the market as I had heard horror stories from friends who had done 10+ interviews and not secured an offer from a PE shop. Even though there is an unwritten code between the banks and PE funds under which the PE funds will not recruit Analysts out of the banks before they complete the programs, that didn't prevent me from leaving early as I don't think a large PE fund would use my former middle-market firm as a banker so there was no risk in harming a relationship that did not exist.

"I definitely did my homework and took a targeted approach and would recommend that others do the same."

My program actually was supposed to end in another year or so; thus I was not exactly worried about getting a job somewhere. I think that in general, it is somewhat difficult for second-year bankers to get into PE, primarily because at the point when PE shops begin interviewing, second-year bankers would generally be only 2-3 months into their second year. At this point, second-year bankers generally don't have a firm grasp of investment banking and the complexities of deal-making; thus I think the ideal time to leave an investment bank is really during the hiring cycle of the third year, provided, of course, that the Analyst gets the opportunity to stay for the third year. If I were to do it over again, I might have waited a bit longer to see more opportunities and gain further leverage in terms of compensation or performance incentives, but I also left investment banking before my second year was completed, so, in a way, I got an early jump-start in private equity.

If I had waited for the typical hiring cycle (late-August through October) there would have been a lot more shops hiring, and candidates get a lot more opportunities to look at different shops. Getting into PE out of cycle is a bit difficult, just because there are fewer opportunities available and a lot of places have already filled their requirements. Also, by entering the process during the hiring cycle, PE shops are forced to compete against each other to attract candidates, and thus compensation/incentive packages might be more attractive and lucrative.

The Partners with whom I'd interviewed had asked a few technical questions, but none were all that difficult to handle. I suppose there were a disproportionate number of questions surrounding the breadth and depth of my modeling expertise, but there was really nothing that I couldn't answer given that I had intimate knowledge of the models that I presented on my resume. My difficulties arose when asked about tax structures and public equity deals, neither of which I had any experience in, given that my investment banking experience had not encountered either of these scenarios in detail. To these questions, I countered with the point that while I did not possess extensive knowledge about them at that moment, I could learn quickly. The hardest questions came from the firm I ended up with, and involved a full case study, with no advance warning, to assess my ability to think about corporate strategy and value creation on the fly.

I definitely did my homework and took a targeted approach and would recommend that others do the same. I first limited the geographic areas in which I would like to live—New York or Los Angeles—then I focused on the kind of shops—primarily operations-oriented shops where I'd have more of a chance to work with management and look at strategy versus being a pure financier and not having any involvement in the way that management runs their companies. Finally, I wanted to find a bit of a smaller place that was less institutionalized, primarily because I wanted the opportunity to advance within the ranks should I be able to succeed. I knew most of the shops on the West Coast; getting to know the shops on the East Coast was a bit more challenging, but I had a few friends at various private equity shops and investment banks who provided some color on opportunities that I thought were interesting."

CASE STUDY 6
An Accountant Gets In—Later In The Cycle
(see Resume 5)

Although this person came from an accounting background, he had a lot of exposure to private equity and LBOs and was considered a top performer at his firm.

"I came out of Ivy League undergrad in pursuit of a job in either investment banking or management consulting. I had a strong GPA with a concentration in finance and entrepreneurial management. The process for getting an interview at a top-tier investment bank was extremely competitive. As a result, it was proving a bit challenging to find an opportunity in a top program. Also, I was leaning heavily toward Boston and there were limited banking opportunities there. Therefore, in addition to investment banking, I interviewed with a number of consulting firms and the corporate finance group of a major public accounting firm in New York. While it was my preference to work in Boston, I was attracted by the corporate finance opportunity and the firm's compensation model, and ultimately decided to take the job in New York. I was not thinking private equity at all. I simply wanted to work at a place where I would be compensated for hard work. I figured I would grind it out over the next several years and see where it led me.

I ended up in a group that provides corporate finance and transaction structuring support for the accounting firm's clients. It was highly technical financial accounting and my time was split evenly working with private equity firms, corporate clients and investment banks. This was my first exposure to private equity and it definitely got my attention. After about a year or so, I was working directly for the head of the group and he wanted me to get my CPA. The job was already accounting intensive and my interests were in finance. I was much more interested in the investing aspects of what my clients were doing than the transaction structuring issues. As I had learned, structuring was only a small part of the deal process.

My stroke of luck came one day in March of 1998 when I got an unsolicited call from a headhunter. This person represented a private equity firm that had just had a bad experience with an investment-banking Analyst it had hired a few months earlier. Now, they were looking for someone with a unique background, specifically, someone outside of investment banking. They wanted someone hungry; someone who would keep their head down, work hard and hold their ego in check. At this point I was well aware that I was not the ideal candidate for a PE firm and that I was off-cycle, but I was intrigued and took the interview.

The first few rounds of interviews were grueling. I had never built an LBO model from soup to nuts, but I believed that I understood how. After all, I had spent the last two years advising clients on purchase and leveraged buyout accounting. My background gave me the ability to read financial models and follow the flow of funds through the income statement, balance sheet and cash flow statement. During the interviews they drilled me hard on financial modeling. I was candid with them about what I knew and didn't know. I also told them that I was confident I could build a model, but I had to convince them of this. The entire process for me lasted about four weeks—it was clear the firm was in a rush to hire someone after their experience with the last person. I think this firm saw in me someone who brought a different perspective, with no pretensions. I knew the learning curve would be steep, but it was steeper than I thought it would be. There were a lot of late nights the first several months and I spent a lot of time calling friends who helped me through some of the trickier parts of the models.

"In my case, the biggest obstacle was that I did not have the customary requisite experience. The PE firms are so used to hiring i-bankers and consultants; they had a hard time under-standing my background."

In my case, the biggest obstacle was that I did not have the customary requisite experience. The PE firms are so used to hiring i-bankers and consultants; they had a hard time understanding my background. I also didn't fully understand the debt markets and other aspects of the deal process, but knew I could learn that quickly. I would definitely say that the traditional route is still the absolute right track to get into private equity and will lead to the highest success rate. I would also advise that people interested in private equity do their homework. A great shop doesn't mean great people. Speak with friends and colleagues who have worked at, or with, various firms to get their sense of the personalities in the organization. Go to their web sites, read the trade rags and see what the funds invest in. When and if you get into a banking group, start to look at PE firms that invest in your area of expertise. Traditionally, it's hard to go from an industrial background to a media buyout shop. So if you happen to get stuck in a group that you don't like, you should try and change, otherwise you could greatly limit your opportunities."

CASE STUDY 7
Directly Out Of Undergrad—An Exception
(see Resume 6)

Here is that exception to the rule—someone who was a star undergrad, did all the right things and landed their dream job straight out of undergrad.

"I made it into a private equity shop directly out of undergrad largely because I was able to get differentiated experiences before I graduated that enabled me to talk intelligently about the industry. A lot of luck helped as well.

Although I graduated in '99 with a degree in history, I got great experience while I was in school by interning at a start-up tech company during my sophomore and junior years. It was a classic start-up and I got a view of all of the different pieces of the business. The CEO there had worked in private equity, so all I heard about was how great an industry it was. From then on, I wanted to work in private equity and he helped me think about how to get into the business.

I spent the spring semester of my junior year studying in London. Following my studies I landed a summer internship with the London office of a consulting firm that has an affiliated buyout fund. I was happy to get the consulting experience, but really wanted to get exposure to the PE/LBO side, so I pushed a bit within the firm and ended up working on screening buyout deals all summer. I thought the finance experience would be a good complement to the tech background I got with the start-up, and I was willing to do anything—endless sets of comparables, blind competitor calls, you name it. At the end of the summer the firm offered me a full-time job after graduation. I wasn't ready to move to London, so I turned it down. Instead, I began fishing around in the U.S.

I knew I didn't have the skill set of someone coming out of an investment bank, but I could talk the talk of the industry (or at least a bit of it), and I had a great story about why I wanted to work in private equity that was backed up by solid internships. I interviewed all over, and was offered a job by a firm that does hire sporadically directly out of undergrad.

A few things stuck out in the interview process. First, the fact that I was able to speak the language of the industry was a huge advantage. The interviews quickly moved off of resume questions into discussions on private equity, recent deals, and the differentiation of the firm, which I think helped.

Second, preparation was essential. Before interviewing, I networked with alumni from the firm who gave me a sense of what to expect. Most private equity firms have web sites where they give extensive information on their investments and the backgrounds of the people. I walked in with info on every person, thoughts on potential areas for investment, and opinions and questions on recent deals the firm had done. That gave me a lot to talk about in meetings and I think probably stuck out. Finally, having a clear, credible story on why I wanted to be in private equity was critical, and being able to back it up with experiences on my resume showed I was serious.

I spent the first two years doing nothing but cold calling CEOs of privately held companies looking for possible deals. I knew that guys in PE hate to teach (or are too busy) so I plugged away, learned financial modeling on my own and eventually moved into more of a deal role.

My advice to other undergrads (and even some MBAs) would be to step out of the campus recruiting mindset of 'I'm going to do the resume drop, and hope the job will come to me.' If you want a job at a place that doesn't hire all the time, or even one that does but where your odds are low, you've got to create your own opportunity. Find a non-traditional way to get in front of people at the firm. Network and lean on friends and alumni. People will respect a cold call or letter if it is done in a high quality way, and many folks will take that call and will appreciate you doing what you can to get into the organization. Often they will make introductions to people at other firms as well.

> "Lots of talented candidates have a high GPA, good test scores and a good banking internship, but no coherent story as to why they want to be in private equity. That will not set you apart. Be ready with your 'I'm-dying-to-get-into-PE' story."

Second, I'd say you've got to have a unique story. Lots of talented candidates have a high GPA, good test scores and a good banking internship, but no coherent story as to why they want to be in private equity. That will not set you apart. Be ready with your 'I'm-dying-to-get-into-PE' story. Show them you have a burning desire to work in the industry and where on your resume they can see the evidence that you're developing skills that are required."

CASE STUDY 8
From Industry Into A Healthcare Fund
(see Resume 7)

This candidate did not have an investment banking or consulting background. He used his science background combined with his corporate experience to land a job with a firm that was launching a healthcare fund.

"I graduated from an Ivy League school in 2000 with a degree in biology. Up until my senior year I had planned to go to medical school and had never thought about finance or private equity. However, after spending several summers working in developing countries with relief agencies and volunteering at the university hospital, I realized that delivering healthcare went beyond medicine, and also involved finance, management and operations. I graduated in 2000, and like many of my peers, I turned down an offer from a healthcare consulting firm and joined an early-stage software company. Once I found out that the company was to be acquired, I began looking for a new job.

I received an offer to run the national chapter of a healthcare nonprofit that I was involved with in college, but turned this down as I had made it to the final round of one PE firm that hired candidates right out of undergrad. Unfortunately, I didn't get the job. So, now I was unemployed with a degree in biology and one year with a software start-up under my belt. I knew banks and consulting firms had a hiring freeze, so I looked in the mirror and asked

"I wouldn't recommend that everyone who wants to go into private equity do it the way I did. But, I would advise that when targeting PE funds, people should target a narrow subset of funds in which they fit. Taking a shotgun approach will not work."

myself, how was I different from other people looking for a job? I decided to target biotech companies and probably contacted every one in the Bay Area. My new job was to find a job, spending eights hours a day sending out resumes, cold calling and researching opportunities. Several months later, I landed a strategic planning role at a well known biotech company launching new cancer products. I picked up basic financial modeling skills giving me some hard skills to complement my operations experience.

I spent two and a half years at this biotech company. During this time, I became involved with a nonprofit venture philanthropy fund that linked business professionals (primarily VC/PE folks with nonprofits). Realizing that I didn't want to spend my career at a large biotech company, I started thinking about opportunities in PE again. I studied the PE industry, used the contacts from the non-profit and also called a recruiter. All the PE/LBO funds I contacted wanted either people with an MBA, two years of banking or, on occasion, consulting experience. They didn't see the value of someone who only had 2-3 years of operating experience. The VCs that I contacted all wanted people with 15 years of operating experience. There was no clear path for someone like me. I even began to think that maybe I should go into a banking program or maybe business school. I was quickly advised against b-school from friends who said I would have a hard time getting a summer job in PE and without that I wouldn't be any better off with an MBA.

I wasn't targeting many funds, but did know that one that had posted a job opening with my recruiter was hiring because it had closed a new $650 million fund that would invest exclusively in healthcare companies. During one interview one of the Partners asked me point blank, 'We are meeting with someone from McKinsey and someone from Goldman Sachs. Why should we hire you?' I admitted to him that my weakness was that I didn't go through a two-year banking program and that I had no hard core deal experience. However, I pointed out that I had been on the company side of deals and could bring a unique perspective having actually worked on the inside of a biotech company. I also told him that he already had people with banking and consulting backgrounds. I had not done LBO/M&A models, but I did understand valuations. I guess he saw my point and I think he was willing to add someone with a different perspective for the new fund.

I wouldn't recommend that everyone who wants to go into private equity do it the way I did. But, I would advise that when targeting PE funds, people should target a narrow subset of funds in which they fit. Taking a shotgun approach will not work. I would also say people should do as much background homework as possible to know the range of opportunities open to them. The 2-2-2 path may give you the highest probability of landing a job, but you will also be going against every Joe Banker. I believe there is a lot of value to getting operations experience early on as it's hard to go back later in your career and get it. Bankers are often viewed as financiers, but not as people who understand businesses. If you only have operations experience it will be a tougher road so you have to be persistent. You have to convince firms why they should hire you instead of a banker."

CASE STUDY 9
From Industry To Buyouts
(see Resume 8)

This is what we would consider an A+ candidate with strong industry/corporate development experience. It is an example of a wildcard—a person who a large LBO fund can hire to balance out the skill sets of the candidates it brings in from traditional investment banking programs.

"I finished college in 2001 with a degree in computer science. I had an extensive tech background and was a summer intern in Microsoft's operating systems group, where I was a software design engineer. Outside of technology, I also did a lot of personal investing and financed my college education with proceeds from my own stock trades. After leaving college, I was looking into management consulting or a return to Microsoft. Except for my personal investing I had no finance background so I didn't consider private equity or investment banking. I was basically a tech guy with an intuitive understanding of business.

I ended up going to Microsoft because they gave me a unique opportunity to do something different. They gave me a chance to play a key role in an internal start-up that had a high amount of executive exposure and potential impact within the company. After two years at Microsoft I thought venture capital was where I wanted to go, thinking it would be a good combination of my business knowledge and technology skills. I called a few recruiters and ended up working with one who pushed me in the direction of private equity.

"When I interview investment banking Analysts, the ones who come off as passionate investors do very well. It's critical that people come off as principals."

Upon interviewing with the individuals in my current firm, I was very impressed. They were an order of magnitude more intelligent and thoughtful than the people I had met at Microsoft or during my undergraduate experience. Despite my inclination for venture capital, private equity seemed to be a place where I would not only learn a great deal of core financial skills, but grow through being pushed by and surrounded with other excellent people.

Despite telling the firm I really had no financial modeling skills, they liked me enough to make me an offer and I took it. Unlike an investment bank, PE firms don't take the time to train you. The thinking is 'you're a smart and motivated guy; you will do what you have to do to get to the other side.' I spent my first two months with my head in accounting and finance books learning how to model for LBOs, etc. My first year was really tough—I understood technology much better than my peers, but really knew nothing about finance, M&A or PE. I think the key thing that clinched the job for me was that they saw someone who was very technical, had done a lot of high-level business thinking, had an intuitive sense for business and had a passion for investing—I definitely played up those factors during my interviews.

For a long time I thought I got the better end of the deal. Someone who comes from an investment bank might not have the business judgment that I had, but they will have the core finance and modeling skills, investment banking polish and acclimation to intense workloads that I did not. I've learned an amazing amount and grown leaps and bounds in private equity, but the beginning was very tough and the two years I've been here have been a long and steep learning curve.

I would say that anyone looking to get into PE should at least get the core financial modeling skills before they interview. More importantly, I would also say to everyone, even those candidates who do have the modeling skills, they should follow the industry, know the numbers and have opinions on deals in the market. They should read things like The Daily Deal and know what is happening. When I interview investment banking Analysts, the ones who come off as passionate investors do very well. It's critical that people come off as principals.

My net advice if you really want to do private equity is: go to a good college, get a high GPA and get into a top-tier banking program. It may sound trite, but that's really the only way to get a realistic and repeatable way of securing a job in PE."

chapter V

From Business School

As a current business school student, you're approaching a major crossroads in your professional career. This is when you hope that all your years of hard work and schooling will pay off. Some of you will use your MBA to solidify a career in private equity that began taking shape several years ago. Others of you are hoping that the degree will be the elusive ticket you need to break into private equity. Either way, if you're passionate about private equity and are committed to getting into the industry (or back in if you were there pre-MBA), now is the time to prove that you belong.

Whether you worked in PE pre-MBA and are looking to continue your pursuit of a career in the industry, or if you are seeking to break into a principal investing role for the first time, the guidance in this chapter will help you understand what you are up against. Since the mix of professional and academic backgrounds across MBAs is so varied, it's difficult to give one-size-fits-all advice to MBAs as a whole. At the same time, giving specific ideas to MBAs based on what they did pre-MBA and where they go to school would fill the pages of an entire guide. So, instead, we will focus somewhere in the middle and follow the general lead of the overall hiring market, which segments MBAs pursuing PE into two major groups—those with prior PE experience and those without.

The Case Studies later in this chapter are also divided into groups of MBAs with and without pre-MBA PE experience. Those in the first group illustrate the relatively smooth return to the industry, but also indicate that the return should not be taken for granted. The Case Studies of the MBAs in the second group confirm that although the process can be arduous, getting a post-MBA job without prior PE experience is not out of the question. If you are in the latter group we strongly recommend you read these stories carefully. Rather than accepting that there was a cookie-cutter approach to getting a job in PE, each of these candidates blazed their own path, made it through round after round of interviews and eventually came out with a coveted job offer.

Pedigree First

Post-MBA positions are generally assumed to be career track and come with a bigger commitment from the hiring firm and, thus, naturally have a high hurdle to entry. This is why when looking to fill these roles there is an overwhelming, if not absolute, preference to hire MBAs who have already worked and proven themselves in private equity. At least initially, most funds will try to hire MBAs who worked at a top firm, excelled there and went on to a first rate business school. These are the obvious stars, the A+ candidates who have the highest expectations attached to them. Hiring firms see these MBAs as top performers who can step in and hit the ground running by adding value from day one. They are seen as future leaders of the franchise. And, just as when they hired at the pre-MBA level, PE firms know exactly where to find these candidates. At the pre-MBA level the leading investment banking programs were the major suppliers of talent. When it comes to finding the best pedigree MBAs, PE firms need look no further than the three to five leading business schools (we list those later). PE funds know exactly what they are getting with these MBAs—proven, experienced professionals from brand name schools and brand name firms with little risk or uncertainty that they will not be immediate contributors.

Glocap Insight

Private equity is like any other exclusive club: once you've been in, it's easier to return. At the MBA level, being "in," means having worked in PE before business school. MBA candidates with a background in PE have an obvious advantage to returning after they finish business school. We can't stress enough that if you're an outsider, meaning you had no PE exposure as a pre-MBA, just landing an *interview* with a PE fund will be a challenge. Getting an *offer* will be extremely difficult.

The Hiring Cycle

As the private equity market has continued to grow and mature, a hiring cycle has developed at the MBA level similar to the pre-MBA hiring cycle we described in Chapter IV. Just as they did for pre-MBAs, at the post-MBA level PE funds will compete early and hard for the best talent. If you're at one of the top three to five business schools and have previous PE experience at a brand name fund, you can expect to hear from funds that are hiring (and even recruiters) soon after you unpack your bags from your summer break. You could even get multiple calls as the funds scramble to beat their competition to the top talent. Your interviews could be condensed into a relatively short sprint.

Unfortunately for the hiring funds (but fortunately for candidates), historically, there have not been enough top-pedigree candidates from brand name funds to go around. So, once that pool of talent has been exhausted, the PE funds reach a point at which they have to decide to look at alternate pools of candidates. This is when the choices become tougher and the process a little more encouraging as there is a more of a level playing field. It's when PE funds are willing to widen the scope of MBA programs from which they seek candidates with previous PE experience and begin to consider some select candidates who haven't previously worked in PE. This trend, which we expect to continue, has opened the door for those MBAs without previous PE experience to potentially take opportunities away from MBAs who followed the traditional path. In fact, we have found that most top funds would admit that given the choice of a B grade candidate who has PE investing experience and an A+ candidate who has no prior PE experience, they would probably choose the latter.

The interview process for the other MBAs with PE experience and even for those without pre-MBA PE may not take hold until later in the year, and when it does it will be more of a rolling one (as were the interviews for later cycle pre-MBAs) but from start to finish it could be quick. In either case, we recommend that all candidates start as early as possible so they are ready when their time comes. The author of Case Study 13 had the right attitude when he said, "On day one, all I worried about was getting a job two years down the road."

In general, the larger, pre-eminent, more institutionalized PE funds that have predictable hiring needs will buy the resume books and/or conduct on-campus interviews early in the first semester of your second year of business school. Most of these funds will initially limit their interviews to those MBAs with prior PE experience at the two or three leading schools, but that is not to say that there is not top talent at other

Glocap Insight

The business schools that are the most recognized national feeders into private equity are: Harvard Business School, the Stanford Graduate School of Business and the Wharton School of the University of Pennsylvania. Following those three there is a group of schools that consistently places MBAs into PE funds. The schools in that group include: Northwestern University's Kellogg School of Management; Columbia Business School; the University of Chicago Graduate School of Business and the Tuck School of Business at Dartmouth. After those, there are several additional programs that each year may also send some graduates into PE. These include (in no particular order): UCLA's Anderson School of Management; The University of Virginia's Darden School of Business; MIT's Sloan School of Management; The Fuqua School of Business at Duke University; New York University's Leonard N. Stern School of Business; The McCombs School of Business at The University of Texas at Austin; the University of Michigan's Ross School of Business and the University of California at Berkeley Haas School of Business. This list should not be viewed as a comprehensive one. Rather these are the schools whose graduates we most often see getting into PE.

leading business schools. Middle market funds tend to recruit more during the second semester as their needs are not often as predictable as the larger ones. There is also a steady stream of funds that interview throughout the year for a variety of reasons and these can be of any size. They can be hiring mainly as their needs unfold. They could be looking to replace someone or coming off a recent fund launch (we've seen firms close $1 billion funds in January begin their MBA recruiting in February) or even because they were too swamped to dedicate the time to recruit candidates earlier in the year. Even though they may begin interviewing later, many of these funds are generally recognized, successful firms that are still going to be selective and will offer attractive opportunities.

The Market & The Competition

Although getting a post-MBA job in PE is still extremely competitive, it's relatively less competitive than it was in prior years. This improvement is a direct result of the continued record amount of money that was raised by private equity (specifically buyout) funds, in 2005 and 2006. As mentioned, the dramatic increase in capital caused PE funds to step-up their hiring to find mid-level professionals to help deploy the fresh capital effectively. But, PE funds found the pickings were slimmer than in years past. According to our research, for the 2007 MBA class there were anywhere from 225-300 MBAs with PE experience at the top 10-12 feeder schools—about 50-75 fewer than in previous years. Further compounding the drop in candidate supply was the hiring activity of hedge funds. In 2006 hedge funds also had a very successful year of fundraising that led them to compete for and hire some of the top MBAs who had previous PE experience—much to the frustration of many notable PE firms.

We expect the momentum in the hiring market to continue at least into 2008 and probably a couple of years thereafter—all signs point to 2007 being another strong year for fundraising and for hedge funds to continue to compete for and lure away top PE talent. However, to be clear, we are not implying your job search will be much easier, especially if you lack previous PE experience. Unfortunately, the stark reality is that there are simply not enough positions available for everyone who worked in PE before business school to return (assuming they want to go back). That means MBAs who worked in PE pre-MBA will be competing amongst themselves for the shortage of available roles as well as against MBAs without prior PE experience who will be pulling out all the stops in an attempt to edge out the experienced candidates.

MBAs With Prior Private Equity Experience

If you're in the elite group of MBAs who worked at a brand name PE fund prior to business school and are at one of the top three feeder MBA programs, a job should be waiting for you when you graduate. However, you still have to identify the best opportunity. That may include deciding if you want to return to your pre-MBA firm, join a large institutional fund, a spin-off, or perhaps a middle-market fund. As each of these options has trade-offs, it will be up to you to decide which is best for you. At this point you may want to skip to the Case Studies and then to Chapter IX, where we discuss the trade-offs of different funds.

For other MBAs with pre-MBA experience who are coming out of a quality but maybe a less brand-name fund, the odds are still in your favor to return to PE. As we noted, the game is all about having experience before business school and you've been playing the game correctly. Based on current market information, however, you would be right to stay focused and not wait for the offers/funds to come to you. Landing a job in private equity out of your banking or consulting program was a great first step, but it doesn't guarantee you a job after business school because the skill set funds look for is different at the post-MBA level. If you haven't taken advantage of business school to further develop your professional skills you could fall short.

> ### Glocap Insight
>
> Over the past few years we've found that about 75% of graduating MBAs who worked in PE before business school return to private equity. We further estimate that 15% choose hedge fund positions over returning to PE. That leaves us with a remaining 10%, who seem to end up taking corporate, consulting or banking positions (potentially as their second choice). Indicative of the strengthening market, we anticipate that the percentage of MBAs taking corporate, consulting or banking jobs may decline over the coming years as the demand for top candidates from PE and hedge funds increases and some of those people successfully find PE jobs.

Given the supply/demand mismatch, your main challenge will be to maintain your edge while in business school. That includes developing additional skills that will convince a PE firm that you are Partner material. You will need to have gained the maturity and investment judgment that can make you a great investor. Ideally, PE funds want people who can step in as a Senior Associate/Vice President and hit the ground running with the ability to generate fresh investment ideas, put together a comprehensive investment thesis and execute a deal from start-to-finish.

While in business school it's also imperative to not only maintain, but continue to build, your network of contacts. In addition to wanting people that understand the industry in which their fund invests, PE funds expect MBAs to have developed an up-to-date Rolodex (one of the reasons you went to business school in the first place) that will hopefully include contacts who can be resources in originating deals and doing deeper due diligence. Some larger funds that have bigger deal teams and make multi-billion dollar investments with several different moving parts will be focused mainly on making sure you have the skills to support complex deals and manage the investment process. On the other hand, smaller funds that may hire once every four years may have a different focus. These funds may need someone with all those similar signs of Partner potential but who can step into a bigger role and who really wants to do smaller deals.

Avoiding The Pitfalls

To maintain your edge you should position yourself in the best light possible so as not to slip through the cracks. Of the MBA candidates who have faltered in their attempt to return to PE, we have identified two common pitfalls—losing focus and being complacent. Regarding focus, we take the simple view that if you like the type of investing you did before business school and you were good at it, there is no need to make a change. Just keep going in that direction and you should encounter little resistance. If you try to go in too many directions you might get tripped up. It's fine to try new things but you should do it for the right reasons so you come across as sincere.

The second pitfall to avoid is complacency. While the odds are in your favor, now is not the time to sit back, relax and assume you will be invited back. You would be in for a surprise if you think you can simply go into an interview, brush off your pre-MBA interview script and get an offer. A lot of other people in business school have PE experience and are going to fight for the available opportunities. Even in the best cycles there is no certainty that there will be enough positions for every person who wants to return.

The Summer

Hiring firms will definitely pay some attention to your summer experience and will want to see that you made good use of the time. We see the summer as an ideal time to expand your knowledge by trying something different (see Case Studies 10 and 12). For example, working at a hedge fund/in the public markets or working in industry to learn company operations are common summer experiences and are generally looked upon favorably by PE funds. Doing something too safe—such as returning to the banking or consulting realm if you've already had that experience pre-MBA—could work against you.

> **Glocap Insight**
>
> For MBAs with previous PE experience, our estimates show that of those who remain in PE, 20% return to their summer employers. Of those transitioning to hedge funds, almost 90% have summer hedge fund experience. About half of those who work in hedge funds over the summer accept offers from those employers.

Trying consulting if you were a banker and banking if you were a consultant is sometimes done. Some people also spend the summer with their pre-MBA PE firm, especially if they want to return. It may not expand your network and skills substantially, but it will be beneficial in providing insurance for you to return. It's probably safe to say that if you do anything other than operations or some form of buy-side, you will probably be asked why you made that choice.

MBAs Without Prior Private Equity Experience

Not that it needs repeating, but as someone without PE experience, you're not in an ideal position. You're at least missing the middle step of the traditional 2-2-2 path and you can't go back in time to make up for that. However, the good news is that each year we do see people get into PE who didn't work at a PE/LBO fund pre-MBA. As you will read in the Case Studies, they do it with some good hustle, initiative, ingenuity, creativity and an unrelenting drive to succeed. To join that group, you will have to possess at least the requisite finance/deal skills and be prepared to prove that to hiring firms. If you have those skills but lack that "extra something special" (which our clients sometimes refer to as the "winning factor" or "x factor"), and the raw ability to be successful and compete, you will not go far. Your objective is to have the hiring firm look beyond any deficiencies in your background to see the unique star qualities you offer so they want you on their team.

As someone without PE experience you have to know where you stand in the pecking order. If you're at one of the top three to five business schools some funds may select you if you dropped for an interview, but those chances increase later in the year as the candidate pools thin out (Case Study 14 does a good job describing the interview cycle for a current MBA without prior PE experience). Although you may get some on-campus interviews, in general, you'll mostly be on your own because PE/LBO firms typically only invite those with PE experience when they come to campus. Almost all of the people that we've heard beat the odds did so by aggressively taking control of their process. A good example is Case Study 17. Rather than sticking to a standard approach, this person set out on an ambitious search that eventually led to a successful outcome. Interestingly, although he came from a top business school he successfully fought through a bias against his school from the fund that eventually hired him. In many ways, this person, like the people in the other Case Studies, succeeded because he showed more drive than his competition—those with PE experience.

Glocap Insight

We look at MBAs without previous PE experience as professional football teams would view a walk-on candidate who never excelled in a Division I football program. Just as NFL teams never *have* to look at walk-ons, PE firms do not need to look beyond the top business schools to find qualified candidates. In fact, they can afford to focus only on a small subset of candidates at those top schools— candidates who have previous PE experience. But both football teams and PE funds do look at "walk-ons" because they know there is the potential to find a hidden all-star.

We recommend that you focus on those PE funds that have set a precedent for hiring MBAs without prior PE experience. If you're not at a top feeder business school, your options will be more limited, but don't lose hope. From our experience, not all PE funds are focused on hiring from the top five or so business schools. In fact, some smaller, regional (and very successful) funds may even have a bias *against* those schools. If you go to the Web sites of funds in cities such as Minneapolis, Dallas, Atlanta, etc., and read the bios of the investment professionals you will probably see that a portion of them are not from the usual brand name MBA programs. Instead, many may have more regional undergrad and MBA backgrounds. In general, firms like to hire what they know. In that scenario, if the funds are familiar with local schools or if they went to a particular MBA program and valued how they beat the odds and what they bring to the table, they will most likely be willing to consider someone whose background resembles theirs.

The Summer

Unlike for those with previous PE experience, your summer could play a crucial role in getting you a step closer to PE. If you're still in your first year it's time to pull out all the stops to get the hands-on principal investing experience you need via a summer internship or by working during school. You may have some deal or project experience from the advisory side, but to really enhance your prospects you need to get PE/buy-side know-how while at business school. It may seem early, but the first week of school is the ideal time to start looking for that position. We recommend using any means available to you to secure some type of summer PE job.

Although getting a summer PE internship doesn't put you on an automatic path to a post-MBA position in PE it does have its benefits: you will be seen as having been able to make another tough cut, it will help you decide if PE is for you and if you are good at it. You may even get invited back by that firm for a full-time job. And, having that offer will be an asset as you pursue discussions with other firms even if you don't intend to accept it. In a hiring market as competitive as PE, we believe that a Summer Associate position on your resume could be enough to get you on the shortlist of candidates who will get a look from PE firms (or perhaps recruiters as well) which is the first step to getting interviews.

Some business schools and professors, especially those outside of the major metropolitan geographies, tend to have good relationships with funds in their geographic area. Regardless of where you're attending business school, you have to be proactive in building relationships and getting in good with your professors could be beneficial in many ways. We recommend casting as wide a net as possible when searching for a summer position and that means using geographic flexibility to your advantage. Try focusing on a top fund in a less-targeted locale such as Atlanta, Cleveland, Dallas, Denver, Miami, Minneapolis, etc. Stay focused on getting the best experience knowing that spending 10 weeks of the summer in an out-of-the-way city is a small price to pay if it increases your chances of getting a full-time position after you graduate.

> **Glocap Insight**
>
> From what we've seen, the MBAs without previous PE experience who fared best getting into the industry after graduation were the ones with two to four years of investment banking/consulting experience plus a summer PE internship.

If you find yourself coming up short in your search for a summer PE internship, there are some alternatives that you can pursue. One is to work for the best, brand name investment bank or consulting firm you can. They generally have respected and influential alumni in PE who can help open some doors down the road. Getting into those top places will at least check you off as validated from a top institution. Next, we would say try to get any buy-side-type role (corporate M&A can have similar characteristics) with a company in an interesting industry. For example, someone who did M&A for a tech company and closed interesting, successful and complicated deals could draw the attention of a tech fund. In the same vein, someone who worked at a major automotive company doing M&A in China could be interesting to a PE fund looking at opportunities involving exporting manufacturing to Asia or a fund involved in a turnaround or distressed situation.

> *Insider Tip*
>
> **PRINCIPAL AT A PE FIRM**
>
> "If you want to get into private equity you have to focus on being an investor, an entrepreneur, an owner and an operator. If you do that and realize that the rest of the skills are a commodity you will show people that you bring value to the table. Financial modeling is important, but it's like a tool in your toolbox. Funds don't want someone who can simply put a model together. They are looking for someone who can think about the results they get out of a model. That is how you can really add value."

Unfortunately, if you are a second year MBA and do not have summer PE experience, the odds are severely against you. You have few choices at this point other than to double your networking efforts with school alumni (we've found that alumni networks are strong in smaller cities) both at the undergrad and business school levels and with your professors, as any strong recommendation could carry weight with a fund.

CASE STUDIES: MBAs WITH PRE-MBA PE

The first three Case Studies are MBAs who followed the traditional 2-2-2 path in banking, PE and business school. Although they all had the appropriate experience before business school, they never assumed their return to PE was a certainty until they had an offer in hand. Each also enhanced their options by trying other things during their summer. We recommend all candidates read these stories, as these are the MBAs against whom you are competing. They had the turn-key investment experience PE firms want and got jobs because of it. After reading these, ask yourself two questions: Do you have what it takes to get a job ahead of someone with that background? And, do you have the energy to devote to going after it knowing the low probability of success? The next set of Case Studies will show you the creative ways in which some people who lacked the traditional background got into PE. The resumes that correspond to these Case Studies can be found in Chapter X.

CASE STUDY 10
Returning To Your Pre-MBA Firm
(see Resume 9)

Wouldn't it be nice to accept an offer from your pre-MBA firm early in your second year? This candidate did and having that offer allowed her to experiment a bit while at business school.

"For me the traditional 2-2-2 path led me right into private equity. I've seen a lot of people move into PE and doing it this way was definitely the easiest route. I finished my Ivy League undergrad in 2000 with a degree in Economics. During the summer before my senior year I interned at an investment bank in New York. Without that experience under my belt it would have been harder for me to get into a banking program after graduation as I had no connections on Wall Street and was not a real finance type.

I ended up at a firm that specialized in M&A and did some work with the restructuring group. This particular firm was short on teaching but good on deal experience. I worked on several live deals, but, unfortunately, not many closed deals. I did learn how to model and the restructuring experience was pretty rare and gave me a bit of a competitive advantage at some PE firms.

"Looking back there is not much I would have done differently. Once you know you want PE and get into the traditional path, things pretty much go on autopilot."

I began interviewing at the end of the first year of my Analyst program and I relied exclusively on headhunters. The people at my firm also helped out with contacts in the PE industry. I found the whole process demoralizing, but luckily I had a backup offer to stay on at my firm for a third year. I ended up taking an offer at a larger PE firm. I interviewed at about 15-20 firms in total. They all pretty much asked the same questions: How do you get to free cash flow? Walk me through an LBO that you worked on. How would you model it? They grilled me on my deals asking if I thought they were good ones—basically anything on my resume was fair game. I think this is a weak point for people with banking backgrounds. They are used to burying themselves in the models. They have to learn to take a step back and judge the entire deal. Some gave me quantitative brain teasers and all asked, why do you want to go into PE? I would also add that since the PE firms don't train you they will expect that you got your training from your Analyst program and they will test that during the interviews.

Being a woman, I also wondered if I was being treated differently since fitting in is so important. I felt this especially at the small firms. If they were only going to hire one person it seemed that the attitude was that it would be more of a gamble on their part to hire a woman. Having one woman in a small group of men might raise the chance of a personality conflict.

I ended up accepting an offer in June, when my program was about to end. Even though this firm didn't require me to go to business school after one year at the firm I decided to pursue my MBA. I was promoted at the end of my second year right before I went to business school and could have stayed on, but I felt I needed a break from working. The firm didn't think there was much value to me going, but they said they wanted me to come back after I graduated.

Having that offer in my back pocket allowed me to go to b-school with a different mindset than my classmates. I knew I had a job to come back to. I was always interested in operations, so, during the summer I took a job with a leading computer company. It was a great opportunity, but in the end I knew it was not for me.

Looking back there is not much I would have done differently. Once you know you want PE and get into the traditional path, things pretty much go on autopilot. I would recommend that undergrads be careful of the group they go into at the investment banks. Modeling-heavy groups such as M&A and financial sponsors will prepare you better for PE than will industry-specific ones. I would also say that those interested in PE after business school should do anything they can to get even a little PE on their resume. Since there are so many people at business school with PE experience most firms are not interested in hiring someone with no PE experience for full-time positions. Having even a little experience from the summer or other internship on your resume will give them something to grab onto."

CASE STUDY 11
Returning With Narrow Geographic Preferences
(see Resume 10)

This person (MBA 2006) also had an invitation to return to his pre-MBA PE firm, but he chose to look around and ended up moving to another fund.

"Given that I had PE experience prior to business school I knew I was in a better position to get a job in PE upon graduating from business school. In fact, I ended up accepting an offer in November of my second year, which allowed me to relax a little bit the rest of the year.

My path into PE began at an independent middle-market investment bank in the Midwest. After graduating in 2000 from a university in the Midwest with a major in finance I went straight into an investment banking Analyst training program. At the time I knew I wanted to be in finance and knew that i-banking was what every high achiever was doing. It didn't take long for it to become clear to me that a great next step for me would be PE. I definitely wanted to work fewer hours than i-banking and I wanted something that was less advisory and more on the principal side. I also knew that I would need another job before business school.

All of my friends had done 2-3 years in an i-bank and then another 2-3 years in a PE shop or other place so I thought that was the way to do things. I had an offer to stay at the bank for a third year, but I began interviewing for PE jobs in October of my second year. Basically, I wanted to work in Chicago and made a list of all the PE firms in that city. I contacted all of them, interviewed with eight and got an offer in mid-January. Some of the bigger firms at which I interviewed had structured pre-MBA programs and a dedicated person doing the first round interviews. Others used a recent business school grad.

At my firm, a traditional leveraged buyout shop, there were about 10 others in the pre-MBA group. About 75% of my time was spent doing modeling work, due diligence and attending management meetings. During the rest of my time I did more proactive deal sourcing work. We all knew this firm never really promoted people without an MBA and that we would be there for two years, three if we did well. I did get an offer to stay on at my PE firm for a third year, and because of that I applied to two of the top business schools, figuring that if I got in I would go and if not I would stay on for the third year and then apply to four or five schools.

When I got to business school, I was about 65% certain that I would go back to PE. I pretty much had a standing offer to go back to the firm where I worked before b-school, but I didn't think I would go back, mostly because of two cultural things that bothered me—I didn't like the hyper competitive nature of the senior Partners and the large number of vice presidents, which would make moving up to Partner difficult. I wanted to go somewhere where they saw *me* as a Partner.

I spent the summer between my first and second years working at a hedge fund in New York, basically to see if I would like something outside of PE. I knew that if you have PE experience pre-business school there is basically nothing that can adversely affect you, unless you spend the summer on the beach. I didn't like the hedge fund business as much as PE. I prefer the deal process and more teamwork.

"I would also say that starting your job search early is critical and that goes for people with or without PE experience. I thought by starting in September I was early, but I wasn't."

I jumped right into my job search in September of my second year. I targeted three cities where I wanted to work—Denver, Los Angeles and San Francisco and generated a list of firms. I treated the search much as I did my search for a PE job during my second year of Analyst training. I methodically called each one to see which were hiring. It took the entire month of September to get through the list and find out which ones were looking for Associates. I only did one on-campus interview as the firms that came to my school tended to be from New York. One major advantage I had because of my prior PE experience was that the firms that did come to campus came to me instead of me having to go to them. All the PE firms would get a hold of our resume book and sort candidates by those who had experience. I would get calls and e-mails from the funds asking to interview me. Those same firms almost never posted jobs so you would only get an interview if they contacted you after scanning the resume book. I found four firms that were hiring and even made one trip to the West Coast on my own dime. I accepted a position on November 10th and could relax until my September start.

Most of the interviews were pretty similar and I would say that people should be prepared. Only one firm gave me a case to read and prepare notes. The rest would have me walk through my background; ask about what deals I had worked on, why I wanted to work in PE and why with that specific firm. The fact that I had worked at a hedge fund in the summer, but was seeking a job in PE also came up at every interview. Some also asked questions like, 'If you had money to invest, where would you put it?'

I would say that if you don't have PE experience it is absolutely critical to do an internship, even at a small asset management shop or a hedge fund to get some buy-side experience. Looking back, knowing that I really wanted to pursue PE after school, I probably should have been more honest with myself and looked for a PE job in the summer. I hadn't interviewed for a PE job in two years and, if nothing else, it would have been good practice. I would also say that starting your job search early is critical and that goes for people with or without PE experience. I thought by starting in September I was early, but I wasn't."

CASE STUDY 12
Straightforward Pedigree MBA
(see Resume 11)

This candidate tried venture investing and operations during the summer, but preferred PE. Even though he had an offer to come back to his pre-MBA firm he still interviewed around.

"Having private equity experience before business school was a major advantage for me. I was pretty sure that I wanted to go back into PE and I had a standing offer to go back to the firm where I had worked before business school. That was a big deal. Some of my classmates who worked in PE before school didn't have a good experience at their firm so they would be searching for a new firm. I could relax a bit and use my summer to try something new.

I wasn't too different from many others who took the traditional path into PE. After graduating in 1995 from an Ivy League college with a degree in Economics, I went straight into an investment banking Analyst program. At the time, I barely knew what PE was. Fortunately, I was placed into the leveraged finance group which gave me exposure to the large LBO funds as I worked on senior debt and high-yield offerings for LBO sponsors. During my two years I got good experience in financial modeling, capital structures, cash flow generation and leverage statistics. It was also at this time that I became familiar with the path to get into PE. I knew that having PE experience before business school would make it a lot easier to get back into the industry after getting my MBA.

I started looking for a job in PE halfway into my second year. Back then the process of getting into a PE shop did not begin as early as it does in today's market. Still, it was a rigorous process. The firms knew I had the finance capabilities, now they wanted to see my thought process on the deals I had worked on. They wanted to see if I could articulate and present deals to an investment committee. The firm I ended up with did a wide range of deals including venture, growth equity and buyout. I also liked the culture of the fund, and this is important because you want to feel good where you work and have a good fit. This firm had a strong mentorship culture and the investment philosophy meshed with my own. I

"During my second year of business school, having the prior PE experience made getting interviews much easier. At our school, all the buyout firms get the resume book and screen the candidates. Without PE experience on your resume you most likely would not be picked for interviews."

had an offer to stay on for a third year and the firm offered to pay my way through business school if I stayed, but I was accepted into what I deemed was a top school and couldn't turn that down. Still, the firm made it clear that the door was open for me to come back.

As I entered business school, my thinking was that PE is a great career path and that I would probably go back, but I wanted to see what operations roles were like. I spent the first 10 weeks of the summer between my first and second years working in an operating capacity at a major Internet company and the next six weeks at a VC firm. The operations role was interesting, but I found that it didn't have the same breath as PE.

During my second year of business school, having the prior PE experience made getting interviews much easier. At our school, all the buyout firms get the resume book and screen the candidates. Without PE experience on your resume you most likely would not be picked for interviews. It's too bad. I think firms lose out by not looking at people with varied experiences, but that is the nature of the beast.

I had an open door to come back to my original firm, but I still interviewed with a few other firms. If you do this, be careful. You can bet that someone will give a reference call to your old firm and they will not like to hear that you are interviewing at other firms. To avoid this, I was selective where I interviewed and told them I had an outstanding offer. I also knew that no one would make a reference call until the later rounds of interviews and I ultimately didn't take any final round interviews. For me, it was better to go with a known firm than to try something different."

CASE STUDIES: MBAs WITHOUT PRE-MBA PE

The people in these Case Studies are the exceptions. They had the winning formula to beat out MBAs who had the sought-after pre-MBA experience. In general, they used an aggressive, multi-pronged strategy which included tenacity and creativity. One person traveled around on his own dime to interview at PE firms that might not have invited him on their own. Why not do the same? You paid $75,000-100,000 (or more!) for your MBA. You should be able to justify another couple thousand dollars if that helps get you in front of people. It may mean flying across country without a scheduled meeting or driving several hours to knock on the door of a fund in which you're interested, but it could be worth it if it bolsters your case. Knowing his limitations, another person took a targeted approach and only contacted the funds where he knew he could add value.

Nearly all of these candidates probably utilized their entire roster of contacts, including professors, school alumni and colleagues from previous jobs. Above all, they would most likely say that they worked endlessly to get what they wanted. You must be willing to take the same approach. To emphasize how challenging it is for most people, we also present the case of someone who tried to get into PE, but came up empty (Case Study 19). The resumes that correspond to Case Studies 17 and 18 in this section can be found in Chapter X.

CASE STUDY 13
Relentless Approach, Early Start

Knowing that he lacked the requisite PE background, this person from the '06 MBA class pulled out all the stops. First, he secured an ideal summer internship. Then he used his extensive network to land an interview.

"I graduated from an Ivy League school in 2000 with a degree in Economics. While at school I did two summer internships—one at bulge-bracket investment bank and another at a consulting firm. After graduating I took a two-year position with a leading consulting firm. Since I knew I would be done after two years I had time to plan my next stop and I wanted that to be in private equity. I always thought I had a mind for investing and putting money to work, but I still liked business and being around companies. I knew econ majors were good for PE and wanted to work with private companies.

Unfortunately, my timing wasn't that great. I began interviewing with PE funds right after 9/11. I also only focused on PE funds in my hometown, which had a limited group of top-tier PE funds (less than 25) and ended up interviewing with six of them. None had the need for a pre-MBA Analyst. So, I thought, why not work in industry? I got a job with an Internet company doing M&A and corporate strategy. The job was very light on financial modeling and accounting, but I worked with our CFO to source acquisitions and develop the appropriate financial and strategic analysis. I also worked with lawyers, bankers and accountants. When I left this company I could not build a model or do much accounting, but I still had a quasi buy-side experience.

I still knew that I wanted to work in PE, but was well aware that I was looking more and more like a consultant/operator. I decided to go to business school and targeted one of the top schools that I knew had a great brand name, strong alumni network and a good track record of getting graduates into PE funds. Before I even got to business school I focused on getting a job in my hometown (not a major financial center). I created a spreadsheet of all 25 firms in this city and loaded it with all my contacts (through my undergrad college, consulting firm and business school) and every bit of information I could find about the firms using my own research and other sources, such as Capital IQ.

I knew one of the first things I would have to do is get summer PE experience. By November 1, I was sending e-mails and making calls to all the people on my spreadsheet. I wasn't specifically asking for a job, but more introducing myself, telling them where I went to school and asking if I could meet them for lunch. All of them said they don't do summer internships and they also thought my lack of PE experience was an issue and therefore I would be a risky hire. It was now January when most of my friends were securing investment banking and consulting interviews and I was still coming up empty. But I continued to send e-mails, make calls, have lunches and even offered to work for free over the summer just to get into the PE industry. Then, a nice thing happened. I got a call in April from one of the PE firms that I had contacted back in November offering me a summer position. It was nice to see the efforts of all my e-mails pay off. I ended up knowing only a few people in my class who got summer PE internships, but it was very aggravating to not know what I would be doing until April.

> *"You've got to expect that 99% of the people will say no to you, but all you need is one to say yes."*

The internship turned out to be a great experience. Since it was a small PE fund ($50 million with only two MDs and me) I got to build buyout models, look at new investments, work with portfolio companies and learn the business inside and out. I ended up working for this fund during the first semester of my second year while I was back at school. It was a real teaching type internship and now when I went on interviews I was able to credibly talk about the deals I had worked on and the models I had built.

My search for a post-MBA job still focused only on my hometown city. Only two funds from that city came to campus to interview, so I hardly checked the job bank. I did have friends who also lacked PE experience and I'd say that for every 25 funds that came to campus they would get 1-2 interviews. We learned very quickly that 2006 was a great year for recruiting. All of our classmates with PE experience pretty much got jobs with their old firms or new ones by the beginning of the year. My friends and I without experience wondered when the funds would find time to start looking at the "riff-raff." Even though I didn't have experience I got a few on-campus interviews because of the work I put in. Figuring that the same firms usually come back to campus, I looked at the list that had come to campus the year earlier and reached out to the ones that were appealing to me. It worked; I got a first round interview at the firm where I ended up getting an offer.

I was still 100% focused on my one city. Fortunately, I got an offer from my summer firm, but I still looked at other opportunities. I interviewed at another firm that claimed they didn't care if you had PE experience. They asked me to talk about my deals, the merits of the companies, how I structured debt and equity on specific deals and what types of companies I liked. They gave me a case study on the merits of buying a plumbing products company. Then I interviewed at one more fund. This was the most intense interview I ever went through, but I was thankful for that. I figure if you don't have experience, but have gotten smart on your own, a rigorous interview will work to your advantage. It gives you an opportunity to prove yourself. I went through four rounds with this firm and there were about seven case studies mixed in. This firm brought in 50 people for first round interviews, all of whom were from three of the top schools. Five people were brought back for second rounds and four for third rounds. My guess is I was the only one who lacked pre-MBA PE or hedge fund experience.

For the last phase of this interview process I was given one week to prepare a major presentation on an investment opportunity. The firm gave me 1500 pages of public filings on the company. I would guess I worked 6-8 hours a day and put together an extensive model and a 20-

page PowerPoint presentation for this firm's investment committee. This exercise was the best thing for me. It let me compete head-to-head with everyone else on a level playing field and I was able to show them that I was the best out there.

I think I was able to beat out others who had experience by working harder on the final case study. I'm sure I spent two or three times the amount of time on it than those I was competing against. The firm even told me that my recommendations and analysis was very compelling. In addition to having strong references I was helped by some softer intangibles. This fund was in my hometown so they knew I would be there for the long term and I had been talking to them for a year so they knew how committed I was.

My advice to other MBAs who lack previous PE experience would be to be patient during your first year and the beginning of your second year, but to work hard networking and start early. You have to be willing to make phone calls and send e-mail and have the attitude that all you need is one person to offer you something. On day one, all I worried about was getting a job two years down the road and I didn't let rejections bother me. You've got to expect that 99% of the people will say no to you, but all you need is one to say yes. I would also say not to expect to get too many on-campus interviews. Networking is the better way to go and that includes talking to friends, reading the industry publications and staying up to date with current events. You've got to be able to talk the talk of private equity. My summer experience ended up paying off for me. I'd say that anyone without PE experience should do what they can to get in the door. Why not offer to work for free during the summer? Volunteer to do a side project during business school, write a white paper or do deal analysis. You need something to set you apart."

CASE STUDY 14
Exhibiting The Winning Factor

Note how this person did not back down despite knowing that it would be extremely tough to find a job without the typical experience. Instead, he got aggressive and his efforts were rewarded.

"My Ivy League undergrad degree in economics led me into a tech banking job at a high-profile group in a bulge-bracket firm. After two years I was asked to stay on as an Associate and ended up in banking for 3 1/2 years before switching over to equity research for six months prior to business school. I did banking for four years, but I knew I didn't want to do that for the rest of my career. I had run hard for four years and decided to go to business school because I wanted to learn other parts of business that I wasn't as exposed to including operations, marketing and leadership. At this time private equity was in the back of my mind, but I was more interested in venture capital, which I had more exposure to while I was in tech banking.

Once I decided to go after private equity job opportunities, I realized quickly how difficult it would be. I was at a top business school and many of my classmates had PE experience. So, not only was I competing against top students, but they were top students with the experience that I did not have. I took courses on restructuring and investing, but many firms could not get around the fact that I had no PE experience. I tried for a summer internship, but there are very few available. So instead, I did a consulting internship and enjoyed that. Consulting gave me an understanding of businesses and organizations on a deeper level and confirmed my belief that working with companies to create financial and operational value was what I wanted to do. I never got picked for interviews out of the resume book, but I started to understand what they wanted. I spent several months researching the industry so I could understand the business. I knew I had a lot of exposure to deals on the research side and was aware that deal skills are a commodity. With that in mind, I spun my leadership skills showing that I was competitive and could manage people. I tried to explain how my experience as Captain of my college sports team taught me leadership and commitment. Through that example, I showed that I was not afraid of putting in time to achieve a goal. I got some interviews at PE funds during my second year, but I only made it past the first round on a few occasions. It always came back to the same thing—I had no PE experience.

I knew my options were limited, but I also knew I could get a job. I got aggressive and worked my network setting up informational interviews with high level people at PE funds and even at operating companies. I wanted to get on people's radar screens. I probably spent a few thousand dollars flying and driving myself around the country meeting anyone in the industry. I saw the money as an investment in my future. And, while I was going on informational interviews I loaded my schedule with other interviews at VC firms and with friends of friends who are operators and had worked with VC firms. Those meetings helped me to refine my interviewing skills.

An opportunity came in February when a fund posted a job listing at my business school. The fund asked for a case study, which I did. I spent quite a bit of time on it feeling that I had to prove something and needed some kind of an edge. The interviews lasted through March and I got the offer in late April. I think I benefited because the firm wasn't on the East Coast, which is a more popular destination for my classmates. In addition, I think this fund was more open-minded about non-PE

"I also sold them hard on my consulting/equity research experience, which demonstrates how, while not making actual investments, I had to make investment recommendations based on my analysis and research."

backgrounds. I worked hard to convey my desire to be in that city and that I was not a flight risk. I also sold them hard on my consulting/equity research experience, which demonstrates how, while not making actual investments, I had to make investment recommendations based on my analysis and research.

The whole process was tough. April was very late in the semester to get a job offer and I knew I was going against 20-25 business school classmates, at least half of whom had PE experience.

I would say that the sooner you know you want to get into PE, the better. Looking back, I probably would've tried to get into PE after my banking program. That path is the easiest way to do it. If you don't take that route, you should definitely work your network (meaning you have to have a network) and try to convince people to take a risk on you. You must also educate yourself about what the firms do and understand the nuances of their investment strategies. Finally, you have to understand how to market yourself in your resume as it pertains to the industry. Put simply, you have to sell yourself and your skills."

CASE STUDY 15
The Benefits Of Networking

This person made good use of his summer to make up for his lack of PE experience.

"Upon arriving at college, I was planning on pursuing a career in medicine and studied science at school. During my senior year, I decided that medicine was not the career for me and wanted to focus on business. Because I had a pre-med background and hadn't taken a business class, I thought the best entry into the finance world where I could learn the most and still maintain a healthcare interest would be an Analyst position on Wall Street. The investment banks had vigorous training programs and an intense work environment where I could learn the needed business and analytical tools. Fortunately, I was able to secure an Analyst position in the healthcare group at a top-tier investment banking firm. As an Analyst, I had great deal exposure, including direct interaction with the venture industry through private placement issuances I had worked on. In my third year, I was able to join the financial sponsors group, which gave me exposure to the LBO world through client interactions and transactions. Honestly, I didn't even know the VC and buyout world existed before I went into banking. I was offered a direct promotion to Associate, but I had decided that my goal was to move to the buy-side at either a buyout or venture firm. I decided to go to business school more because I had never taken any finance classes and thought this would be a great way to round out my business education. I also thought it would make me more attractive to the PE industry.

> "Strategy-wise, I believe it's important to target the right funds given your background. You shouldn't waste your time or the funds' time looking at places where there will not be a good fit."

I enrolled in several VC/PE classes in business school and participated in the VC club. I also took advantage of my school's internship program, which allowed students to work with a local company during the semester for credit. I completed one internship with a VC firm and another with a small start-up biotech company. The internships gave me direct VC and small company exposure. For my career, I decided to focus on VC because I thought my scientific educational background and healthcare financial experience would make me a more attractive candidate to a VC firm than a buyout firm. I felt that the buyout shops were looking for someone with more M&A experience which unfortunately I didn't have.

I went back to Wall Street during the summer between my first and second years of business school—it was 2001 and VC firms were not hiring, not even if you offered to work for free.

My job search began in October of my second year and took about nine months. I networked and contacted every one I knew from my past work experience, internships and my own personal contacts. The networking definitely paid dividends. I think finding a job without networking will probably be based more on luck, simply being in the right place at the right time. The 2-2-2 path into PE is absolutely the best way to get into buyouts, but not necessarily true for VC. One obstacle I faced, that pertains specifically to healthcare VC, was not having a PhD or MD. However, as one moves from early stage investing to later stage and into the LBO world, the advanced science degree becomes less and less important.

Strategy-wise, I believe it's important to target the right funds given your background. You shouldn't waste your time or the funds' time looking at places where there will not be a good fit. Knowing what I know now, if I had to repeat the process all over again, I would probably have done my two years at a VC or buyout fund before going to business school. In my case I had an opportunity to go straight from my banking program to a VC fund, but I wanted to get business school out of the way. Having the two-year experience at a private equity fund before business school makes it much easier to pursue a career on the buy-side after school. And based on the number of firms that have these two year programs in place, it seems that it's now almost becoming a necessity."

CASE STUDY 16
Taking A Targeted Approach

This person may not have made it if he hadn't identified the fund that was best suited for him.

"After graduating from college, I spent two years teaching high school. I then earned my joint degree in business and education. I decided to pursue private equity while I was in business school—I had taken some private equity classes and thought that it was an excellent field to hone one's understanding of business fundamentals. I was hoping to move to New York after graduating, and heard of a private equity firm that invests in education and training companies from one of my professors. I thought it would be a good way of combining interests in education and business and getting a different experience than I had as a teacher.

I do not think I was in a very good position to get a private equity job with minimal business experience, and received some good advice from a counselor at my graduate school: do a research project for the private equity firm as an independent project for credit. The firm suggested that I do a project on financial aid options outside of federal aid, and it worked out well. Still, they said they weren't hiring anyone. Eventually, we worked out a deal where I would work there for the summer. After that, they appreciated my work and offered me a permanent job in the fall. At first, my role was largely market and legislative research, but since then I have become a true investment professional—building models, working on transaction details, etc.

If I were intent on a private equity career earlier on, I would have gone the i-banking route from the beginning. In my case, though, I would not have done anything different to set myself up for the job. I do not think my firm will seriously consider a younger candidate from a non-traditional background. I think the only way to get a job at this firm if you have not been in PE or banking (or had officer-level experience at an education company) would be to do something that gave them solid proof that you were bringing something to the table: conducting a substantial research project, bringing in a deal, coming to them with a specific, well-thought out investment idea."

CASE STUDY 17
Going After The Job In Person
(see Resume 12)

The efforts of this candidate are a prime example of going the extra mile to get what you want.

"I finished undergrad in 1998 and went straight into a two-year Analyst training program in the M&A group of a major New York-based Wall Street firm. After the two years I was promoted to Associate, but instead got into a top business school and decided to go, making me one of the younger people in my class. From day one, I began thinking about how I could get into private equity. I knew that private equity is a challenging, dynamic industry and I wanted to be an investor rather than an advisor.

Unfortunately, my timing for securing a private equity job was as bad as it could be. Just before entering business school the Internet bubble burst and the economy fell into a recession and most Wall Street i-banking firms and many PE firms were simply not hiring. With only a banking background, I knew I had to get PE experience somehow. I lined up a summer internship at a small private equity firm, but it was rescinded two weeks before I was to start because of the downturn, leaving me with nothing to do for the summer. I called a former MD from the M&A group with my former employer. He had moved to Tokyo to strengthen the firm's

M&A practice and asked me to come out for the summer. I didn't want to go back into investment banking, but I wanted something to do for the summer so I joined him.

When I returned for my last year at business school it seemed that everything was stacked against me and my goal of working in private equity: I had no private equity deal experience, I was young and people were asking me why I went back to investment banking for the summer if I really wanted to be in private equity! I was set to graduate in 2002, again the lowest point in the economic downturn with many of the top tier Wall Street firms instituting hiring freezes, many for the first time that anyone can remember! In February of my last year I received an offer from an investment bank to work in their M&A group in London. I didn't necessarily want it, but it gave me something in the back of my pocket while I searched out my "dream" private equity job. I was able to put the firm off until April (which was no small task) while I did what I could to get a job in private equity.

> *"I decided to take the same approach to my job search that I knew I would use when, and if, I got a job in private equity. I wouldn't wait for the job (or investment opportunity) to come to me."*

I decided to take the same approach to my job search that I knew I would use when, and if, I got a job in private equity. I wouldn't wait for the job (or investment opportunity) to come to me. Rather, I began contacting firms myself. I targeted the entire country. I was open to most any city because the market was so bad. Finally, I made a cold call to a middle market investment banker in the city where I went to college and he said I should call the CFO at a local PE fund. I did. The fund wasn't looking for anyone, but I knew they were raising a new $450 million fund. So, I made a point of visiting my college buddies, calling the fund professionals in advance and asking if I could stop in. I probably repeated this trip four or five times beginning in November. It wasn't so bad since I liked visiting my friends and there were several world class ski resorts within close proximity. Ultimately, they said yes, we want to hire someone but asked me "Why should we hire you?" They were adamant that they didn't like my business school and that, even though I went to school in this city, I wasn't from there. It took a lot of convincing, but they finally said, "We like this guy," and brought me on. I was very honest with them from the beginning and admitted my major weakness: I told them that if they had come to my business school to interview MBA candidates, they would have found many more experienced people than me. However, they should look at me as a longer-term investment and that I have proven in my past experiences to be a quick learner.

My advice to others would be to treat your job search as if you are an investor looking for an investment opportunity. As an investor, you are looking for companies that are under the radar screen. When I targeted funds I looked for ones that others hadn't discovered yet. I thought if a mid-market fund could raise $450 million in a small market then it must be good. On top of that, it had first class investors, solid investments in interesting industries and a good, but very limited, reputation. I didn't let my lack of private equity deal experience deter me and I think my attitude, willingness to work, general fit and likeability eventually got me the job.

Needless to say my decision turned out to be a terrific one. The economy began to turn and there was, and continues to be, a robust environment for buying and selling companies. It took roughly two and a half years for the firm to invest most of the new fund which provided me with a firehouse of activity, both on the buy- and sell-side. Off the back of this heightened level of activity and broad experiences I was fortunate to land a Principal level position with a very successful middle market PE firm in NYC."

CASE STUDY 18
Taking A Pre-MBA Role As An MBA
(see Resume 13)

Knowing full well what he was up against, this candidate took the unusual step of accepting a pre-MBA job after business school.

"I had a somewhat atypical background going into my search for a private equity job. After graduating from undergrad in 1999 (Bachelor of Science in Physics with Distinction and a Minor in Economics) I worked for two years in the technology group in the San Francisco office of a mid-tier M&A boutique turned semi-bulge bracket via acquisition. I got little actual deal experience given the market timing of this position.

I went straight to business school after two years at the bank. Once I was in business school, I started thinking about getting into private equity and was focused on doing something in the San Francisco Bay Area. There were no summer positions available at private equity firms, so I decided to try for a summer job at a top investment bank, which I got. I made an effort to round out my skill set a bit by trying to focus on transactions involving leverage. I received an offer to join full time after graduation.

When I began my private equity job search in the fall of 2003 (which consisted of setting up informational meetings by leveraging the network I had from business school), I was told "no" outright. I had half a dozen or so informational interviews, and people just said, 'You seem like a good guy, but there is no way we would hire you.' They all had too many candidates who had private equity experience. Why take a risk on somebody who didn't? I decided to pursue a pre-MBA job, arguing that I had similar work experience to other candidates they were talking to. Some of the more institutional firms did not accept this idea, but a few of the firms did. At the end of the day, I got one offer, but that's all it takes. I think this firm brought me on for a couple of reasons: a) it is relatively younger and less institutionalized and b) despite my lack of experience, everything else on my resume was strong—3.98 undergrad GPA, promotion to Associate at my banking program, 770 GMAT, First Year Honors at business school and an offer for a full-time position at Goldman. All of that made them more inclined to take a chance on me.

Even though I looked good on paper, I had to know my LBO stuff cold. I had to be sincere about wanting the work, explaining that my alternative was to return to Goldman and that comparing those two scenarios I would learn more in private equity, get paid about the same, and be much better positioned after the two years.

> *"The keys to getting the job were recognizing early that I was passionate about PE. Even though my non-traditional strategy worked for me, I would suggest that others follow a more traditional path before business school. That said, a lot of people find themselves already in business school and then wanting to go into PE."*

I also had to give them the sense that I was mature about the decision and not expecting any special treatment because I was an MBA. Finally, I had to be open about not expecting any full time positions at the end of the two years. I didn't worry that I was taking a step back by accepting the pre-MBA position and it was easy for me to convince them of that because I truly believed that I would get good experience. I was basically reversing the order of the MBA and the pre-MBA private equity experience. After one year at the firm and having performed well I was told that I was expected to stay on after the second year as a post-MBA. My strategy worked!

The keys to getting the job were recognizing early that I was passionate about PE. Even though my non-traditional strategy worked for me, I would suggest that others follow a more traditional path before business school. That said, a lot of people find themselves already in business school and then wanting to go into PE. In that case, recognizing this as early as possible will increase chances of getting a job. Another key was making the decision to go for the pre-MBA job (and demonstrating in an interview maturity and sincerity in taking this position), having an extremely strong academic background (good schools and high GPAs and GMAT) and having an offer in hand from a top investment bank also helped."

CASE STUDY 19
One Who Tried But Didn't Make It

This is the plight of one MBA grad without previous PE experience who couldn't break into the industry. It paints a good picture of what you are up against.

"My work background includes about four years at a major consulting firm (not PE-specific) followed by two years as an Associate on the private equity team of a major corporation's pension group. After business school (class of '03), I tried to find a job at a buyout firm. After talking to many Partners at LBO firms as well as a few headhunters who specialized in these positions, I was told that it wasn't worth my time because I had none of the following: an investment banking/M&A background, strong industry experience, nor any direct deal experience. I was told numerous times that there was such a large supply of candidates looking for LBO jobs who had those skills and experiences, and so few positions, that I pretty much had no chance. I even tried to get a pre-MBA position, but was also told that they preferred people coming out of an investment banking program. My advice would be don't even think of working at a private equity/LBO firm unless you have a good contact with someone at the firm or someone who knows the firm well. Blind resume submittals almost never work."

chapter VI

Post Business School: Experienced Finance Professionals

At this point you are probably set on a nice career trajectory. In all likelihood, you are on a growth track to perhaps becoming a managing director at an investment bank (or the equivalent at a consulting firm) and heading toward the pinnacle of your profession. However, you have concluded that private equity is where you belong, and you're worried that hiring firms may think you are too expensive, too advanced in your career or, most likely, that you don't have what it takes. As someone with little or no direct private equity-related experience you're aware that the window to get into PE was open wider when you were more junior, but you also know that you can't go back in time. There is really no reason for you to switch to private equity, other than the fact that you want to.

You've chosen one of the most difficult times in your career to attempt to get into private equity. At this point PE funds are looking for the next generation of leaders and are resistant to training anyone who is unproven. Maybe you've seen others transition into PE at a similar stage, or perhaps you've gotten close enough to people already in PE to become familiar with what they do. Either way, you believe you have similar skills and therefore think there is little to stop you from making a move to the principal side and being successful. Basically, you've been watching the industry from the sidelines and are itching to get on the field and play.

From our experience, the select people who get in at this stage of their careers are the high achievers who always had the appropriate skills, but never applied them in a principal setting. Most likely they didn't realize the allure of PE until they got to business school or were deep into their careers. We call these individuals "late bloomers" and have included some successful examples in the Case Studies at the end of this chapter. These people certainly didn't *need* to switch careers since they were on the fast track to success in their professions.

To move off the sidelines you will need more than skills and desire. At this stage of your career there is no definitive hiring cycle and no one best path to get into PE. Just as a 25 year-old athlete who still dreams of playing in the Majors has to show extraordinary skills to even get a tryout, so too will you have to demonstrate that you have superior talent to get a look by a PE fund. And, even if you have that ability, you will probably need some help to get that "tryout." From what we've seen that help can come in different forms, including from your clients, senior people at your firm, people in your own network and, in rare cases, a recruiter. Historically, a recruiter's hands are tied. If we get mandates for 10 post-MBA searches and all require five years of previous LBO experience, we have little room to introduce a banker or consultant who lacks that tightly defined specification. It's not that we don't want to help people in your situation or that we think you're not going to make it. It's just that we are limited to introducing only the candidates who closely fit the specifications we are given by our clients.

As you will read in Case Studies 20, 21 and 22, most people say that if they knew there was an easier path that they could have followed earlier in their careers to get into PE, they probably would have taken it. While the stories of how they made it are unique, the authors had some things in common—they were all top performers at top firms, showed an unrelenting determination to succeed and also had fortunate timing. In their cases, since they were too late to take advantage of the traditional path that worked for others, they had to find creative ways to get in front of PE funds while at the same time being star performers. These examples include one person who had CEOs at his client companies make calls on his behalf, another who joined a PE client who knew him and a third who got in by writing a cold letter to someone who was forming a new fund.

Positioning Yourself

If you are truly serious and dedicated to moving to the principal side, you should first make sure you have the answers to several inevitable questions—both for your own self-assessment and for the PE funds with which you hope to interview. You will be asked why you want to get into PE (in fact, that is one of the most commonly asked questions of all candidates and we address that more in Chapter XI). However, in your case, the question could take on more meaning since you may never have worked at a PE fund before. You will most likely also be asked: Why do you want to get into PE now? Did you think about working in private equity before? If so, did you try to get in at an earlier time in your career? What happened? If not, why didn't you try before? Why do you think the timing is right for you now?

Those who did get in at this stage in their careers would probably have answered these questions by saying part of their plan was to work hard to excel and get the most robust deal/project experience so they could move up through the ranks of their firm. Most likely they weren't thinking about how that experience could have helped them move into PE. They would probably be able to honestly say that they didn't know there was a traditional path that they could have followed to get into PE earlier in their career.

If a PE firm is considering making an exception to bring you on, the Partners will grill you until they are satisfied they are making a good choice. Since you haven't cut your teeth in PE, your investment judgment, financial knowledge and deal skills will be scrutinized. In addition, since you would most likely join in a more senior role, PE firms will want to see that you have all the signs of a potential leader. Be ready to admit that while you never did principal investing, you do bring something of extra value to the table that more than makes up for what you lack. If you thought you were good enough to have gotten into PE earlier in your career they will want to know why you didn't. Perhaps you didn't know the path. Perhaps, you went to a regional school or were at a smaller bank or consulting firm where the path was not discussed. It's possible that you took your career in another direction and only found your stride in finance after your first few jobs.

As you embark on your PE job hunt, there are some specific strategies that can help you put your best foot forward. Before you initiate the process, it should be a given that you are a top performer and are most likely at a well-respected investment bank or consulting firm. If you aren't, it will be incrementally more difficult for you to break in and frankly may not be worth the effort.

At this point, getting exposure will be a key to your success, and our first recommendation is to do what you can to make yourself visible to PE/LBO funds. The best way to do that is to get into a PE-related group at your investment bank or consulting firm, if that is still possible. Being in a group such as financial sponsors, leveraged finance, or even M&A (or a comparable one in a consulting firm that works on the other side of LBO/PE deals) will allow you to be viewed as somewhat deal ready by PE firms.

Our second suggestion is to make every effort to get closer to your clients so that they are willing to be references for you (most of the investment bankers who make the transition into PE come from groups that have worked in some way with PE funds and in many cases those bankers ended up joining one of their clients). This is especially important to those bankers and consultants who are not in groups that work with PE funds. Many top CEOs seem to be networked into PE funds, but they will only help out pure all-stars who they believe truly outperformed for them. Maybe the CEO saw the value you created for his/her business and can validate that you can step in and do the same for the Partners of a PE fund. In our experience, bankers and consultants who get into PE without having been in a group that gave them exposure to PE funds are at least fluent in PE deals and therefore able to keep up in interviews.

The third part of your plan should be getting a senior member of your firm to champion your cause. Many people we see get into PE at this point in their careers had Managing Directors at their firm support them, often by placing a call to a PE fund on their behalf (or at least willing to call once a candidate had traction with a particular fund to which they had some connection). Give a thorough read to Case Study 20 to see how helpful a senior person's contacts are.

CASE STUDIES

As we indicated before, these are all examples of people who broke into PE a little later in their careers. For all of them, the combination of being a late bloomer, a high achiever, extremely tenacious and visible to PE firms created opportunities for them.

CASE STUDY 20
An All-Star Banker Makes It

This person didn't go to a top-five business school, but he was a star performer at a top-tier investment bank. Note how he had CEOs and clients make calls on his behalf.

> "My undergraduate degree in accounting led me to a job with a major accounting firm in the audit department. At the time I had heard of a few major LBO firms but was generally unfamiliar with the private equity industry. The accounting job seemed like a reasonable first step to take out of undergrad. I spent four years at the firm and then decided to go to business school. I had become interested in private equity through friends and thought that a post-MBA position in investment banking was the best route to get there. I also knew that an MBA was a great long-term career move regardless of the moves I made immediately following graduate school.

During my second year of business school I made some attempts to learn more about the PE industry, but quickly realized that without prior PE experience it was a long shot. I also learned that banking was not a sure route into PE—banking provides good deal experience, which is a requirement for PE, but there were tons of MBA students out there with prior PE experience and they would get the few available jobs over people without any PE experience. At the time I knew that no PE experience and no real deal experience were my two biggest hurdles. This process also confirmed that the best way to get into PE would be to work at one of the premier investment banks but this route would still be a challenge.

I decided to accept an offer from a premier investment bank during the fall of my second year after spending a summer at the firm. I felt that working for this firm would be a great resume builder and was a better option than toiling for months in the post-MBA PE job market. Given my background, I assumed that if I was lucky enough to get a PE job it would be with a no-name firm that didn't necessarily have a stellar track record—so working for a top tier i-bank made a lot of sense. Before accepting I made some calls to PE folks and friends in the industry. Everyone told me that, for me, getting into PE would be an uphill battle. They all told me to go work for the bank for a few years, so I did.

"Unfortunately, there is no published list of firms that will hire people without prior PE experience so it was a bit of a buck-shot approach to the market."

As an Associate I was in a generalist group doing deal execution, M&A and various financings. I had a long-term interest in PE but was firmly committed to succeeding in banking in the short-term. At the time, my thoughts were 'I'm doing this now and I'll see what it's like. If I like it, I'll stay. If not, I'll look around.' I put the PE search on the backburner. This was 2001 and there was a recession. A lot of my banking colleagues had been laid off so I was happy to have a job. My first year and a half was rough—the markets were bad and deal activity came to a halt. The following 18 months were much better as deal activity picked up significantly and the firm was quite lean thanks to numerous rounds of layoffs. Anyone who survived got good deal experience. We had small teams and I worked on M&A, debt financings and a few PE deals. I got to know people at PE firms and worked with their portfolio companies.

At the end of 2003 I began making calls to assess the possibility of a move into PE. Once January 2004 rolled around, I launched a broad PE search. I made lots of calls—to clients, to headhunters and to friends in the industry. Some CEOs/clients made calls on my behalf and through that process I lined up a few interviews. My understanding was still that to get a post MBA job in PE one would need prior principal investing experience. When I launched my search process people confirmed that my lack of PE experience would be a significant impediment. I also quickly learned that once you are out of business school there is no fluid hiring market—it's more like a spot market where people get hired once in a while. As such you need to be in front of as many firms as possible so that when they are hiring you will likely be on their radar screens. Casting a broad net was important. I eventually found a PE fund that was open to my background. Unfortunately, there is no published list of firms that will hire people without prior PE experience so it was a bit of a buck-shot approach to the market.

For me, being at one of the top investment banks was crucial. It made me (and my resume) stand out, especially because I was a generalist. I'd say if you are a specialist banker, the group you are in is important. There is no doubt that the brand name of the firm that you join is crucial. If you are using the bank as a stepping stone and have choices I would say always go with the best brand name firm even if you do not like the group/people as much. For me, it was an easy decision because I liked the people and the firm a lot.

If I could dial back the clock to when I was 22, I would have gone into banking after undergrad. Taking that path would have saved me a few years. The path I chose eventually led to a position in PE but it was a long process. I would say that building a network is crucial. It's important that you develop a personal rapport with your professional contacts. In my case, my contacts opened doors for me that would have been closed otherwise. In the end, it's a combination of being good at what you do, being very opportunistic and very aggressive and, of course, catching some breaks along the way."

CASE STUDY 21
Joining A Client

This person was a top performer in undergrad and in banking and had an MBA from a top school. He was also able to prove himself over time to his client. He helped his own cause by leveraging his personal and business network.

"My path into PE was definitely circuitous and difficult to manage. I went to a military academy, where I pursued a major in the social sciences. At the end of my five-year service commitment as an armor officer, I decided it was time to go to business school for a variety of reasons. Based on my limited exposure to the private sector at that time, I thought I would follow many of my non-military friends into consulting post business school. It seemed to offer the best training for someone with my background.

Many of my business school classmates had come from PE, and, to a person, all of them wanted to return to the industry. Their descriptions of their experiences and responsibilities sounded exciting, so I continued to learn more. In contrast, those who had come out of banking and consulting didn't seem to have as much enthusiasm about going back.

I soon realized that there was no way I would be able to join a PE firm with my background. Everyone I spoke to encouraged me to do something else in a related field and try to get into PE later. If I was determined to become a PE professional, they encouraged me to work in an M&A group at a leading investment bank first. Even with that addition to my background, my chances of transferring into PE post-MBA with no pre-MBA PE experience were slim.

I ended up taking an Associate position at a top bank, where I was fortunate to work on portfolio company transactions for my current PE firm. Along the way, I asked many folks for general PE career advice. Time and time again, I was told how difficult it would be to make the transition from banking. 'The PE skill set is just too different and your timing is too atypical,' they said.

> *"I set a uniquely high bar for what I wanted to do in PE, knowing that I also would have been thrilled to stay in banking for the rest of my career if things didn't work out in PE."*

When I entered my third year at the bank, I figured it was the last year I could leave without wasting time. An extra year in banking wouldn't make me any more marketable to a PE firm. It was time to focus either on leaving banking or on staying and becoming a managing director. I made the choice to move on. I wanted to work at a late stage, large-scale technology-focused fund on the West Coast. I thought the leadership and management skills I learned in the military, coupled with the deal experience I gained in banking, could be conducive to leading teams of consultants, bankers, lawyers and accountants on complex PE deals. When I met with PE folks during the recruiting process, I asked them to set aside the bias against my banking background and focus on the skills required for success in PE—quantitative skills, analytical rigor, and highly developed process management experience. It took a lot of selling, but it worked out and I joined a West Coast PE firm as a Principal.

The hardest thing was convincing people to interview me. I called 10-20 business school classmates before beginning my search process and I didn't get many words of encouragement. No one thought I could make the transition. When I did see job listings the specs certainly didn't include my background. Even headhunters told me I would have to do it on my own.

If I could go back in time, the only thing I would do differently is stay in even closer contact with more people in the PE industry throughout my banking career. Individual relationships are critical. Building and maintaining those relationships over time—and staying patient and flexible—allowed my search to be successful. It requires a bit of work, to be sure.

In my case, the stars aligned for my current firm to hire at the same time I was looking. It would be hard to count on that happening again. Most important, I wanted to ensure that I was happy with my alternatives. I set a uniquely high bar for what I wanted to do in PE, knowing that I also would have been thrilled to stay in banking for the rest of my career if things didn't work out in PE. While my road to PE may have been eased by doing something in PE before business school, that path perhaps would have been even more challenging. Making the transition from a tank into PE overnight, without any financial background, would have been tough."

CASE STUDY 22
The Bold Approach: Direct Outreach To A Firm

Take note of the especially creative way this person got his foot in the door of a major PE fund. The strategy may not work for everyone, but combined with a little luck the focused aggressiveness and determination are traits that should be emulated.

"I graduated with a degree in English Literature and Religion—not the traditional course of study that someone would pursue to go into finance. I tried to get a job in publishing, but came up empty. I had interned at an investment bank during one of the summers during college and ended up returning to the same bank working on the mortgage-backed securities trading desk. I had never taken an accounting or finance class and had little understanding of what the traders were doing, but the buzz excited me and I wanted to be a part of it.

I stayed at the bank for two years. I could have stayed longer, but I had applied to business school and got in. My plan was to go into i-banking. In b-school I majored in decision sciences (statistics), accounting and finance. I interned during the summer at a different bank and had an offer to come back full time after graduation. Somewhat fortuitously, I met a Partner from one of the leading banks at a high school reunion. He advised me that if I wanted to move ahead in the industry I should work at either his bank or one other, but not the one at which I had an offer. He ended up getting me an interview and offered me an Associate position. I did a wide range of corporate finance work on industrial, real estate, lodging and gaming companies.

My thoughts quickly turned to PE. I didn't like the large institutional feel of a big bank and wanted to get closer to the action. I figured that swapping banking for a principal investing role would put me even closer to the action and away from being just an advisor. No one really told me it would be hard to get into PE.

My fortunes took a turn for the better when I wrote a letter to a leading figure in the world of private equity. I had read that this person was leaving his firm to start a new one. It was a gutsy move, but I wrote him and said it would be great to get to know him. At the time there was no money going into the industrial economy; it was all earmarked for tech and telecom. This person had a similar view on the importance of industrial companies as I did. I wrote that I thought what he was saying made a lot of sense. After sending the letter I harassed his secretary for weeks and finally met with him and his partners. I put it on the line and said I wanted to be an Associate at his firm. It took a lot of coaxing, but I got in. That was six years ago and I'm still working at the firm.

I've had more luck with non-traditional routes than traditional routes. I know that most people get into the business the traditional 2-2-2 way, but I suspect that is because it's the path of least resistance. The fact is the skills that you use in PE are not only those you learned in the banking and consulting programs. Now that I'm working in the industry, from my point of view if we're hiring someone who worked at PepsiCo for two years in corporate development and knows modeling, that person may be more valuable than a pure banker. Over the next five to 10 years I suspect that the hiring focus will change and the non-traditional will become traditional. Candidates should realize that the world has changed. There are a lot more funds. People should do their homework and find out: What are the senior guys in it for? Do they have one fund, or more? Are they good investors? How do they make decisions? And, will you be a part of those decisions?"

> *"I've had more luck with non-traditional routes than traditional routes. I know that most people get into the business the traditional 2-2-2 way, but I suspect that is because it's the path of least resistance."*

chapter VII

Post Grad School: Experienced Non-Finance Professionals

Perhaps you are a lawyer, doctor or accountant or maybe you work in industry. Although you have yet to reach the pinnacle of your current profession you're definitely on that track. Nevertheless, you feel like you have a true sense for business and have decided that you are interested in becoming an investor and want to know if it's possible to transition into private equity and, if so, how you can go about it.

Even though you have probably established yourself in your profession, you may be considering becoming an investor or owner. It's not that you're unhappy in your current profession, but you believe PE may be more appealing and could be your road to long-term career satisfaction. You should know that few people enter at this juncture (the non-Partner, non-CEO level) as they most likely lack any kind of proven investment track record and most requisite finance/deal skills. At this point there is no set pattern, no hiring cycle and no getting around the fact that you're far off any traditional path. Nevertheless, if this is what you really want to do, our aim is not to discourage you. Whether your background is purely legal, medical, accounting or if you are an industry professional, you may be able to argue that you have an important skill set that pure finance candidates don't and which can add value to a PE fund. Examples of these skills could be deep science/industry knowledge (that could come with a good network), business building/turnaround skills, legal skills associated with structuring complex transactions (especially bankruptcies) and forensic accounting expertise that allows for more penetrating financial analysis.

Although there have been some very prominent CEOs who have moved directly into a PE fund (Jack Welch of GE joining Clayton Dubilier & Rice comes to mind), that is not the level we discuss in this chapter. Those types of industry professionals would be able to walk into several PE funds and a position would probably be created for them. This chapter is more about offering ideas on how to transition into PE for people who are advanced in their career but have not reached the pinnacle.

Breaking In

Based on our experience, a good deal of non-finance professionals who enter PE or VC funds do it directly, meaning without taking an intermediate step. We will give some examples of people who got in that way, but it seems that most of them were not actively pursuing a move into PE and benefited from a direct proposal from someone they knew. Those who did not have such good fortune had to map out a longer term strategy to break into PE. In those instances, we found that most lawyers, doctors, accountants and industry professionals who were able to actively plan a future move into PE did so in a couple of different ways, one which we call a "back-door" method and the second we describe as a "two-step" process.

We define the back-door method as using your profession to get a foot in the door at a PE fund (for example a lawyer becoming an in-house counsel at a fund) and parlaying that over time into an investment role at the same fund. The two-step path on the other hand entails first moving to a more direct feeder industry into PE, such as consulting or investment banking, and then stepping into PE. If you are committed to getting into private equity either path would offer an opportunity. However, in our opinion you also have to be ready for it to *not* work so be prepared for the process to take time. You will likely have the most success if you have the mindset that you would be happy staying long-term in whatever intermediate step you take. Most importantly, you could jeopardize any chances of making the switch if you don't allow yourself enough time to excel in your new role.

In our experience, a mid-level industry candidate (below the CEO, CFO, COO, etc. level) with non-tech operations experience has had a difficult time making the move to PE, especially if that person has *only* operations experience (in this chapter we don't talk much about technology industry professionals as they are usually targeted by venture capital funds which are discussed in Chapter VIII). The non-tech candidates who historically have had what it takes to make it into PE are usually those who have excelled in many different categories having substantial success managing divisions and products and helping grow and/or turnaround companies. Take the case of a senior manager at a corporation such as General Electric who may have helped launch several products and grown two divisions while having direct management of a few hundred people. This person wakes up one day and thinks, "I'm an operator. I've successfully built companies just like the PE/LBO guys, and I'd like a share of that upside." They may have the skills to move into a PE/LBO fund, but will have to convince the fund that they can create similar substantial value in a less structured environment and that they are generally worth the risk over other PE finance pros who funds can always take first.

The Back Door

The back door method generally works better for lawyers and senior accountants because they can fill similar internal roles at PE funds. For example, as mentioned, a lawyer could join a PE firm as in-house General Counsel. While you will not be going in as a deal professional you will at least be at the firm and could possibly, over time, develop into such a role (this is by no means a guarantee). Although there is little use for an in-house doctor, an MD could follow this path by becoming a Special Advisor to a healthcare fund and then perhaps a board member of a portfolio company in their field of expertise before being invited to join the fund in an investment capacity. A senior finance or accounting professional at a prominent institution could parlay his/her skills into a role as a CFO at a PE fund and could eventually move investment position. Industry professionals from tech-related fields or entrepreneurs with ⌐ ience can also use the back-door method to get into a venture fund by becoming an ⌐ neur in Residence (see Chapter VIII for a more detailed discussion of that role).

⌐ natter your profession, if you get into a PE fund through the "back door" you should make the most ⌐ it while you are there. And don't rush things. It would be a mistake to go to the Partners of the fund during your first week as an in-house General Counsel or Special Advisor and ask to move to the investment side. They should not be given cause to believe that you have your eyes on another job in their firm. Most importantly, you must be willing and mentally prepared to buckle down, work hard, perform well and make the most of your given position.

We know of an accountant who got in via the back door method. After working at a major accounting firm for five years, this person joined a client—a start-up PE fund—as a controller and then switched to a larger fund that needed a CFO. This fund allowed him to work a little on deals (he was a liaison to CFOs at portfolio companies after deals closed and got some operations experience from those contacts), but his main role was CFO. He eventually received an offer to join another large, well-known fund—also as a CFO. However, he had obviously proven his potential to his current fund and was offered a full-time Associate position on the investment side if he would stay. Needless to say he took it and hired his own replacement CFO.

The Two-Step Process

Another way in which people make the move into PE at this stage of their careers is what we call the two-step process. This can work for lawyers and accountants, but is often also very effective for doctors or industry professionals. In this process someone would first move into an investment bank or consulting firm to learn some of the necessary deal skills and then attempt to transition into a PE fund. Following this path is especially helpful for doctors/scientists as the finance or consulting skills obtained in an intermediate step, in combination with their medical/science knowledge, could potentially make them better positioned to get into a healthcare or biotech fund than would an average career banker or consultant without that additional education (most commonly, the MDs who get in at this stage of their careers were the ones who never practiced medicine). Once you get into an appropriate banking or consulting group, your move into PE will be similar to the route followed by the people we described in Chapter VI.

One example of an MD who we know, moved into PE this way by joining a major consulting firm after his medical training. At the consulting firm, he specialized in pharmaceuticals and medical products and worked closely with senior management of large and specialty pharmaceutical companies. He also focused on alliances in the industry and product launches and then joined a PE firm to work on its biopharmaceutical investments. MDs/scientists may also go through a two-step process by first moving to an industry role. As people who can often be on the forefront of groundbreaking discoveries they may be able to join a biotech or medical devices company right after medical school or getting their PhD. In that way they could get involved in developing breakthrough products and lay the early groundwork to pursue a position at a healthcare VC firm (again, we go into that in more detail in the next chapter).

Examples Of Some Who Made It Directly

We have a Case Study of an attorney who got in directly. Before getting to that, we will include some shorter examples of other non-finance professionals who made it into PE without first taking an intermediate step. Again, given the unique aspects of their good fortune, it's hard to give advice on how to pursue this means of entry, but the stories are worth pointing out. Two things that all these people had in common are that they were all top performers and had direct exposure to the PE industry.

There is the example of someone who was the leading science officer at a major research institute. In addition to having an MD degree, he also had a PhD and an MBA. He was an accomplished author and won awards for his biomedical and technology research. His scientific and research background allowed him to join a PE fund where he focused on biotechnology and medical device companies. Another situation we know of is someone who had an undergraduate degree in biomedical sciences, an MBA from a top five business school and an MD. That background led him to a healthcare VC fund where he focused on investments in companies developing drugs and medical devices.

We have come across some lawyers who got in directly as well. One had a varied background as he worked at a major accounting firm prior to law school. After graduating he spent four years as a mergers and acquisitions associate at a leading law firm. His legal work gave him exposure to PE and he was invited to join a family office structuring and negotiating public and private investments. A second example is that of an M&A lawyer who did a good deal of private equity work at his firm. While practicing law he got to know his clients at an LBO fund and they asked him to join the firm with the understanding that they would train him in exchange for some help with legal housekeeping.

CASE STUDY 23
An Attorney Moves Into A Distressed Shop

The Case Study below is of a lawyer who got into an LBO fund directly after being exposed to private equity for many years.

"Before entering private equity, I spent 14 years working as a bankruptcy and finance lawyer. I became intrigued with working as a principal in a distressed debt private equity investment firm after working with, and sometimes against, a number of distressed debt investors. I thought my legal background in leveraged finance and insolvency would suit me well as a principal with a firm that invests in distressed debt since a major part of the investment analysis requires an understanding of creditors' rights and the bankruptcy process.

"You really have to become known by people in the business who can verify that you know what you're doing."

Fortunately, my law firm was the general fund counsel for just such a fund. And, even more fortunately, the fund was looking for someone with legal bankruptcy experience. This firm was launching a new multi-strategy fund that had a significant target allocation for distressed debt. One of my colleagues at the law firm told me about the opportunity and I approached the PE firm and got an interview. I went through the same interview process that the candidates from traditional business backgrounds went through, which included the preparation of an investment analysis of a company selected by the PE firm. That took a lot of work and required me to come up a steep learning curve. Aside from the relative unfamiliarity of the project, I was handicapped by the lack of access to the financial resources that someone at a bulge bracket investment bank would have. Fortunately, I did well enough on the project for the firm to hire me as a Director. As the firm grew from $800 million in assets under management to $2 billion, I added General Counsel duties to my responsibilities. Now, about 60% of my time is spent doing deal work and 40% is General Counsel work.

The bottom line is it's not easy to transition from law into PE unless you start on it very early or late in your career. And, when and if you do make it, you should know that PE is harder than it looks. Business analysis is different from legal analysis and is not something that most lawyers have experience doing. If you make a mistake, you, and not your client, have to live with the results. Moreover, there is no shortage of lawyers who would like to be doing anything other than practicing law. If you want to shift to the business side, you have to make yourself visible. Your best entree will be through connections, not by throwing your resume around. This is a very clubby world and it is very hard to get in. You really have to become known by people in the business who can verify that you know what you're doing."

chapter VIII

Venture Capital

In the previous chapters we discusssed the career path of later-stage private equity/leveraged buyout and spoke at length about the various entry points. For the most part, breaking into the world of early-stage venture capital has very little in common with getting into later-stage PE/LBO (except that it is difficult), hence we felt it deserved its own chapter. In fact, we could have written an entire book on searching for a job in venture capital, it's that different.

Do you closely follow companies that begin as a couple of people with an idea and become industry leaders? If you do, you can probably not only name the founders of those companies, but also the venture capitalists who provided the start-up funding. Perhaps you are attracted to revolutionary technologies and want to be a venture capitalist who helps discover, fund and build the companies that will comprise the next generation of technology or life science leaders. Maybe, you are even considering working at one of those companies or starting your own. Either way, you may think working at a VC fund will get you that much closer to being an insider at one of these success stories. You know what? You're right—but not necessarily on the same path you may envision. Venture capital doesn't always offer a long-term promotional track as later-stage private equity generally does, but it still can provide a great springboard into other opportunities.

To set the tone for this chapter we will begin with a description of what you can expect from your first role in venture capital. Following that, we will give an overview of what it takes to break into the venture world. We will also outline what it takes to become a Partner, but since that process is so unique we won't touch on it until later in this chapter. We also offer Case Studies—the first-hand accounts of four people who broke into venture capital in different ways. To emphasize even more clearly what VC funds look for when hiring, we thought it would be especially useful to present some job specifications from actual searches on which we worked (you will find these at the end of the chapter).

For nearly all of you who are just beginning your initial pursuit of a position in venture capital, we advise focusing less on the career track and, instead, more on breaking into venture capital in the first place. If it seems that this chapter goes out of the way to emphasize that your first role in venture is less likely to set you on the path to becoming a Partner, it's because that's one of the things that makes venture capital so different than other careers in finance. And it's something that will dramatically affect your future in the industry as well.

Building a career in venture capital doesn't work the same way as it does in later-stage private equity. One of the main pieces of advice we give people looking to build a career in later-stage PE is to get in as early as possible. In venture capital, getting in early is not necessarily the most important requirement. In fact, getting on the Partner track has less to do with an advanced degree (MBA, PhD, etc.) or having a few years of banking, consulting or operating experience. In the venture world, one of the biggest challenges—and one of the themes of this chapter—is that getting in is one thing, but staying in and becoming a Partner is another challenge altogether.

Your First Role

We purposefully don't call this role "entry-level" because we believe that doing so would be misleading, even though this is typically a support role. For simplicity sake we refer to the junior position in venture capital as a "non-Partner" role. Although it represents the first entrance into the world of venture capital, the role should not necessarily be viewed as the first stop on an automatic path to a career in VC.

Regardless of the point in your career at which you join a fund, the actual role is usually very similar—you will source, screen, qualify and structure deals for the Partners and support some of the portfolio activity. However, the level of responsibilities can vary depending on your prior experiences. Nevertheless, even if you take on some very senior responsibilities there should be no mistaking that you are most likely many steps—and probably years—away from becoming a Partner. Except in the rare cases, your initial foray will be a limited one in terms of duration. It could be two years, maybe three or four, but usually not much more.

As you will see in Job Searches 1-3 at the end of this chapter, when VC funds hire at the Pre-MBA level they generally require a few years of work experience with a background in banking, consulting and/or operations as well as a good knowledge of technology or biotech/healthcare/medical devices (also with a preference toward those having engineering degrees). The funds that hire at the post-MBA level implement what we call an "apprentice model." This is also not usually expected to be a promotional role, but given the increased requirements—most ask for several years of operations experience, a deep knowledge of a specific industry, strong finance and market knowledge and at least a Bachelors or Masters in engineering—it's expected that post-MBAs bring more to the table on day one than pre-MBAs.

Glocap Insight

To simplify how we as recruiters look at non-Partner opportunities in venture capital, we break the candidate market into two categories—"pre-MBA" and "post-MBA," however these descriptors are not meant to be literal (you can think of them as "Junior non-Partners" and "Senior non-Partners"). We define pre-MBAs as people who have generally been out of college for five years or less and have spent the majority of that time as the most junior professionals in their organization or team. Post-MBAs are those who have been in the workforce for at *least* five years (sometimes with as much as 10 or 15+ years of experience). They may or may not have gone to business school but, more importantly, have probably moved up the ranks at least once and are starting to take on more mid- to senior-level responsibilities.

Part of the reason it's so hard to climb through the ranks of a VC fund is the general belief that to be a successful venture capitalist you will have to demonstrate consistent value creation over the long term. As you would expect, it's unlikely you will be able to do that while at a VC fund for only a few years. VC firms are simply not in business to keep non-Partners around for 10 years while they try to develop the skill set needed to build successful companies. It is generally accepted that you will have to do that outside of your venture investing role.

VENTURE CAPITAL

AN INSIDER'S VIEW OF THE VC MINDSET

In his essay on *Mastering the Fundamentals of Venture Capital* in *Inside The Minds: The Ways of The VC*, Terry McGuire, co-Founder of Polaris Venture Partners, points out that venture is an intuitive business, which makes an apprenticeship appropriate. He writes that: "Developing an intuition for what is going to work requires exposure to many great entrepreneurs (and many unsuccessful entrepreneurs), many great deals (and many mediocre ones), many promising new technologies (and many that fail to deliver). This takes time; it can't happen overnight. Even when a venture capitalist has done his homework and studies all the objective data carefully, investment decisions boil down to gut reactions." McGuire, goes on to point out that his mentor, Stan Golder of Golder, Thoma Cressey, once told him that "venture capitalists use four parts of their bodies—their minds, hearts, guts, and the seat of their pants. The last three have nothing to do with quantitative analysis. You have to develop a sense for the deal."

From what we've seen, possessing about 10 years of successful operating experience *pre-venture* significantly increases the chances that you will have the tools necessary to stay on, but there is no guarantee. A good example of someone who entered venture capital with significant previous operational experience can be found in Case Study 27. This person has been out of undergrad for 16 years. He has a Bachelors and a Masters in electrical engineering and spent nine years steadily progressing in various industry positions in both product design and marketing roles. He has been at a VC fund since 2001, but his long-term status is still uncertain. As you would expect, the reverse is also true: the less operating experience you have pre-venture, the stricter the two- to three-year commitment will be.

Breaking In: The Process

If we had written this guide 10 years ago there probably would have been little advice at all about breaking into venture capital. Most would agree that, back then, the VC industry was an exclusive group of funds, each of which had not much more than a handful of Partners. The large majority of VC funds didn't have much junior leverage and the ones that did rarely promoted them through the ranks to Partner roles. But, the industry has evolved in many ways—today it's more global, there are more deals to pursue, more companies to research and more conferences to attend. There has also been more capital raised and that has increased the competition to find quality deals. At the same time the scope of technology has expanded dramatically, making it, in our opinion, harder for Partners at venture funds

CHART 7
Evolution of the Venture Capital Market

	1994	2006
No. of VC Firms in Existence	391	1,054
No. of VC Funds in Existence	660	1,818
No. of Professionals	4,210	11,627
No. of First Time VC Funds Raised	16	34
No. of VC Funds Raising Money	128	191
VC Capital Under Management ($B)	35.2	268.4
Avg VC Capital Under Mgt per Firm ($M)	89.9	254.6
Avg VC Fund Size to Date ($M)	40.7	98.6
Avg VC Fund Size Raised ($M)	71.7	199.3

Source: Thomson Financial/NVCA

to maintain by themselves the level of expertise and global coverage needed to find and make great investments. Although the industry remains very clubby, VC funds seem to have succumbed to the need for more non-Partners to provide the necessary leverage to stay competitive and successful.

We estimate that 50-70 VC firms hire at the pre-MBA and post-MBA levels each year. Pre-MBA hiring in venture capital follows a cycle similar to the buyout world (outlined in Chapter IV) as VC funds compete for some of the same candidates—mainly tech bankers and consultants and especially those with an engineering background. At the post-MBA level, VC funds generally hire with less frequency and when they do it's usually with less urgency. In fact, from what we've seen, VC funds rarely "need" someone at the post-MBA level, but at the same time they can always make room for an all-star. We've had venture clients specifically tell us "if a great candidate comes along we'd be happy to take a look at them."

There are few defined entry points at which people generally get into venture capital. Instead, there is more of a continuous spectrum of times throughout your career when you can break in—including pre-MBA, right out of business school and even several years out of graduate school (as in private equity, it's rare that someone enters venture capital straight out of undergrad). The key to getting a VC role is being patient and disciplined. If now is not the right time to get in, you should continue to build your skill set to be better prepared for the next time you pursue an opportunity.

Breaking In: The Skill Set

To understand the skills required by VC funds it might be worth revisiting the differences between early-stage venture capital and later-stage PE/LBO investing. To refresh your memory, PE/LBO funds invest mostly in later-stage, mature, cash-flow producing companies that are usually profitable and therefore more straightforward to evaluate. On the other hand, venture capital funds target companies with little or no cash flow and infrequently use debt in their investments, therefore they put less of a premium on the pure financial modeling and deal skills valued by PE/LBO funds. Venture capital investment analysis focuses on product risk (will a specific product even work?), market risk (if it does work, will customers buy it?) and on getting a company to profitability and positioning it for a possible sale or IPO. VC investing combines deep technology expertise with good financial knowledge, so VC funds target candidates with operations exposure, solid business skills and investment instincts and an impeccable knowledge of the industry in which a specific fund invests.

Given the importance of hands-on experience, VC funds tend to prefer people with direct product management backgrounds—seeing companies from the conceptual stage through to sales. Consultants, who arguably have a good mix of finance, strategy and operations knowledge, are also frequently sought after. Bankers are less emphasized because their strength is in the numbers and deal complexity and venture investing is less about evaluating cash flow and more about analyzing companies and products that may still be in their infancy.

VC funds favor those people with technical undergraduate degrees, mainly in electrical engineering or computer science (most job specifications list EE/CS degrees as a strong preference if not a requirement) but can also include mathematics, physics and biology, etc. A Masters, medical degree and/or sometimes a PhD (usually in the case of healthcare-focused VCs) are also common requirements (see Job Search 5). We have seen people break in and excel without these degrees, but they were able to make up for it by developing a deep expertise in a specific technology as well as having a combination of strategy and/or product management and business development experience (a good example is Case Study 24).

Insider Tip

MANAGING DIRECTOR AT VC FUND

"In 1997 I made an investment in optical technologies for communication applications. I was considering making another 4-5 investments in the space. I had a reasonable grasp of the markets/applications, but wanted to be able to evaluate the alternative approaches (i.e., different technologies) in depth. So I hired a recent PhD, late 20's, who had worked in the business for a couple of years. He had the specific technology depth as well as a flavor for the competitive environment. We scoped it out together. Together, he and I scouted out some of the more interesting/promising opportunities. More importantly we avoided the major "dogs" in the space."

Breaking In: Helping Your Cause

Even if you have the academic degrees and the skills listed above, breaking into venture capital will be tough, however there are ways you can help your cause. First, you must find a way to get in front of VC funds. Although it might seem that finding the next generation of top Associates/Princiapls would be obvious for hiring firms, that is not the case. The star candidates can come from many different places (consulting, operations, banking, research etc.) and be in numerous roles (business development, marketing, sales, etc.). So, even if you are an ideal match for a venture fund, it may be difficult for anyone, including recruiters, to track you down. One of the best ways to get the necessary exposure is to network with as many people in the venture community as you can. Every employment guide probably lists networking among their recommendations, but in the case of venture it can be an essential part of your strategy. As we said, venture is a clubby industry. VC firms do deals together, they work near each other and are often in the same social circles. There are numerous conferences and cocktail parties that are good opportunities to meet people, especially in major tech hot spots such as Silicon Valley. If you get into that network there will be a better chance of someone making an introduction for you.

Another unique aspect of venture capital is that if the Partners of a VC fund think you're good, but have no position for you in the near term they may still want to put in the effort to build goodwill with you (remember club deals are still common in venture, so a fund may see you as a potential deal partner down the road). In that case, don't be surprised if you speak with a VC fund and they tell you, "We're not looking, but I might have someone else I can introduce you to." The VC introductions can also extend to other channels—even recruiters. We frequently get referrals from people in the industry and we heed those recommendations.

One more way you can help your cause is knowing the VC industry basics, including how funds are structured and how they invest. If you are fortunate enough to land an interview, you will probably inhibit your progress if you are not familiar with commonly used terms such as "preferred equity," "Series A and B" financings, "Angel funding," "pre-money," "post-money," "up-round," "down-round," etc. If you don't quite know these terms and their context, we recommend you learn them.

The Entrepreneur In Residence

Some funds have Entrepreneur in Residence (EIR) programs that allow people with extensive operations and/or entrepreneurial experience in a specific sector to break into venture capital. In a 2003 article in the Seattle Post-Intelligencer, Dan Rosen, a venture capitalist with Seattle's Frazier Technology Ventures (and now retired General Partner), described the Entrepreneur In Residence as "one of those terms of ours that covers all sorts of things. In some cases, it is a holding place for somebody who you want to have in one of your portfolio companies. In other cases, it is somebody who helps define your strategy. And, in other cases it really is somebody who has some specific skills that can help your companies in a lot of ways and does short stints with those companies."

Above all, EIRs are encouraged to apply their sector-specific knowledge to pursue new business opportunities. By having an office at the VC firm, EIRs get the support of the firm's infrastructure and its network while also using the investment professionals as a sounding board. In addition to benefiting from having someone with sector expertise in the office, the venture fund also generally has right of first refusal to invest in the start-ups sourced or created by the EIR. EIRs generally stay with a fund for an agreed upon length of time, but there is always the chance that they could be kept on in a more permanent role and there is precedence as some people have stayed on and become fully integrated into the partnership.

I VENTURE CAPITAL I

The Kauffman Fellows Program

It's worth pointing out the existence of a unique program that seems to attempt to level the playing field and help a handful of professionals enter VC each year. The Kauffman Fellows Program is a formal 24-month apprenticeship program designed to educate and train the next generation of leaders in venture capital and high-growth companies. The Fellowship, which began in 1994, combines an intense educational program with individual mentoring from people at major firms in the venture capital community. Each Fellow works at a leading VC firm that sponsors them. The only two unconditional requirements to apply for the Fellowship are that you have a graduate degree in business, science or technology and five years of full-time professional experience (on average, Kauffman Fellows have 10 years of successful operating experience, deep domain expertise in a specific field and a history of proven leadership, according to the program's web site, www.kauffmanfellows.org). Candidates go through a series of interviews in person and then a matching process to pair them up with a VC fund. Although this program offers an alternative entry option into venture capital, the Kauffman fellow usually still has the same potential track as people who get in as a non-Partner in other ways.

Are A Few Years As A Non-Partner Worth It?

At first glance, it may seem that the VC funds are getting more out of the non-Partner role than you, especially if working those initial few years doesn't necessarily set the stage for promotion or an eventual return in a more senior role. However, we don't see it that way and believe there is a quid pro quo and that you would also gain a lot from working at a VC fund. To us, even a few years at a VC fund could open doors to some great opportunities. At the very least you may find that getting into venture capital early will give you an idea about whether the industry is for you—and you could always go back to doing what you did before you got

> ### Glocap Insight
>
> In venture capital you *can* see a company go from five to 350 people, and you could see it happen multiple times. You will also read hundreds of business plans, which will hopefully help you avoid any pitfalls if you start your own company.

in. In addition to the skills that you will acquire, you will also develop an all important network in what we have said is a very tight-knit industry and that alone will benefit you no matter what you do moving forward. There is no doubt that your time in venture will be a great learning experience and there is the possibility that you can stay on at your fund and possibly get on a Partner track.

We are convinced that you will emerge from a few years in venture capital as an experienced technology or life sciences investor and you could use that knowledge to do a host of other different things. Many people consider venture investing a great way to learn how to run their own company. As a junior professional, you will learn best practices for early-stage businesses from accomplished business builders/investors. You will examine countless business plans, help construct term sheets and get exposure to many different portfolio companies. All of this will give you a bird's eye view of how funds are invested, how start-ups raise capital, how CEOs are hired and how deals are structured. At the same time you will be privy to the inner workings of management strategy and product development and will see start-up companies go through several stages of growth.

It's possible that you may identify one of the start-ups that you work with as the next industry leader and end up joining it. Or, if your venture fund considers you an absolute top performer and a value creator, it may be the fund that specifically asks you to take an operational role at one of its portfolio companies, thus keeping you close so they can continue to evaluate your development. We estimate that about half of the people who complete their term at a VC fund after a few years end up in operations to continue

VENTURE CAPITAL

Glocap Insight

People who take a non-Partner VC role do so for reasons similar to people who pursue an internship at the White House. The latter group wants to begin a career in politics, and they know the internship will be a good stepping stone. But they harbor no illusions that they will stay on past the end of their internship. They do the internship because they know they will meet a lot of people, learn how Washington, D.C. works and figure out if politics is for them, but they know they will not stay on and become a senior White House official. In VC, as a non-Partner you know you are being brought on for a limited time, but you also know that you will get a first-hand look at a top operating role, access to the best potential start-ups and potentially an entrée into business school (if you haven't gone already). Candidates who go into VC are also motivated by the desire to gain as many technology community contacts as they can, to understand the different sub-sets of technology better and, of course, the opportunity to see if venture investing is what they want to do in the long-term. Both the pre- and post-MBA roles are for people who love technology or healthcare. They know it will better position them to pursue their career goals—in venture, operations or elsewhere.

learning how to grow and manage businesses and products. Those who were in operations before they entered venture capital will most likely return in a more senior role, with a new set of managerial skills and a better understanding of cutting edge technologies.

For those who don't go into operations and remain on the financial side of technology/life sciences, we have known some who move into public sector investing with a hedge fund or equity research at an investment bank (note: you would most likely not have gained the modeling and deal skills required to join a later-stage PE fund or the M&A group of an investment bank). Some junior professionals who are starting their careers as pre-MBAs may use their time in venture as a stepping stone toward business school. Even if they end up leaving venture capital altogether, they too should be better off from the experience for the reasons we mentioned. We have seen a smaller percentage of the people make a lateral move to another venture fund that values the training of people who have completed apprenticeships at other funds. There's a good chance these people will be on Partner-track at their new fund (see Job Search 7).

Becoming A Partner

Despite all of the challenges we have presented, you might still want to know how you can best position yourself to reach the pinnacle of a VC fund. Some people do enter VC funds as Partners, but they are usually the ones who have had considerable success in business/operations—maybe they launched a few successful companies and took them public or sold them—or are very successful people in other areas (Colin Powell joining Kleiner Perkins is one example). If you're in one of those groups, this guide is not for you. For the others (and that should be most of you) there are few shortcuts you can take to become a Partner.

In a perfect world VC funds would hire people as Partners (or future Partners) who have been involved in full product cycles—conception to commercialization—as well as full company cycles—from start-up to maturity. They would bring on professionals who have been at companies that have grown exponentially and preferably been sold or taken public for a large profit. Not surprisingly, historically many Partners at venture capital funds enter the industry as a second career after having been part of creating successful, profitable companies or profitable divisions of larger companies. Hence the Catch-22, generally, to become a Partner at a VC firm you have to have been very successful beforehand in your career, but if you were successful in building a company and reaped the financial rewards of that you may not need or want a VC job.

Having said that, a more recent trend we have noticed is VC funds beginning to loosen the requirement that people have "substantial" success in industry to be on Partner track. This is all part of the evolution of the market over the past decade. In our experience, VC funds that previously looked to hire non-Partners to mostly manage their deal pipeline are now placing an increased premium on a new generation of professionals who have better access to deals. This, in turn, has opened the door for more people to be on the Partner track in spite of the fact that they may have limited operations experience. Similarly, we have also seen people returning to venture capital after having left to get more seasoning in operations (especially if their first turn in venture was earlier in their career). This further validates the idea that the non-Partner role can be a prelude to an eventual career in venture.

CASE STUDIES

Below are the stories of four people who made it into venture capital. Although each took a different route to get into venture capital—graduating from business school with an entrepreneurial background (Case Study 24), leveraging consulting and engineering experience before business school (Case Study 25), the uncommon course of breaking in with a law degree (Case Study 26) and going through many years of operating experience (Case Study 27)—they all had backgrounds that closely tracked the requirements listed in the job specifications later in this chapter. In fact, the author of Case Study 24 ended up getting the position described in Search 6. At the same time you will see that the first three people don't necessarily see themselves in their current positions in venture long-term. The resumes that correspond to Case Studies 25 and 26 in this section can be found in Chapter X.

CASE STUDY 24
The Advantage Of Successful Entrepreneurial Experience

This person had an undergrad degree in Economics, but got his technology experience at a start-up company. That experience led him to launch his own company, which he grew and eventually sold. He then went to business school before joining a VC fund. He knows that his stay in venture capital depends on how he performs and that even if he shines there are no guarantees he will be promoted.

> "Getting into VC is tough. Most people recommend allocating 6-12 months to look for a job in venture. I got lucky and it took only a few months, but that is definitely not the norm. I had the things that people check off—I work hard, have a good academic background, some banking, consulting, operations and entrepreneurial experience and good references. But there are tons of other guys who have that as well. It's unfortunate, but it's a crapshoot.
>
> I wasn't even thinking about venture when I finished undergrad in the mid to late 90's with a degree in Economics. I did two summer internships while I was in school—one at a private equity firm in Asia and another at a Wall Street firm doing equity research. Econ grads from my Ivy League school pretty much went into finance, consulting or to law school, so I followed suit and began an investment banking Analyst program at a major Street firm. I was in the M&A department focusing on tech and telecom.

Like many others I realized pretty quickly that I didn't want to be an investment banker forever and I left the program after my first year. I saw a lot of friends and classmates doing entrepreneurial things and wanted to do the same. I joined a start-up Internet services firm that did consulting and development work. I saw it as a great segue way into the start-up environment. I was one of the first guys hired into a burgeoning strategy group.

I stayed at the start-up for a little while and then some friends and I decided to start our own company. It was 1999-2000 and the Internet world was in full force. In just a few years we raised equity funding, acquired another company and then sold both pieces of the company. While building a company was exhilarating, I was not sure that I wanted to tackle another one right away. Given where the market was and at this stage in my career, I made the decision to attend business school.

In business school my plan was to start another company. I even thought about taking a leave of absence or leaving school to do it, but for a number of reasons the timing was not perfect. I had been an East Coast person most of my life and wanted to try California, so I worked for the summer at a consulting firm's tech group. After my summer experience in California, I knew I wanted to return and thought that VC would provide a great avenue to build a network, gain breadth of knowledge in multiple sectors and keep me close to start-ups.

"After my summer experience in California, I knew I wanted to return and thought that VC would provide a great avenue to build a network, gain breadth of knowledge in multiple sectors and keep me close to start-ups."

Getting into VC is a lot different than PE and the process varies from firm to firm. I know some people with 1-2 years of experience at an I-bank or a tech company, some of whom are younger than me, and they are on the Partner track (after having proven themselves). I know others who are older than me with more experience but are not on the path to becoming a Partner. I've learned that the earlier stage firms want more operating/ entrepreneurial experience, while the later stage firms are more willing to take guys with banking and consulting experience. Of course, all venture firms would love to get guys who started billion dollar companies so the single best way to get into VC is to start a really, really successful company.

Market timing also has a lot to do with hiring. At any one time there may only be a few venture firms actively looking to hire. If a good guy comes along, most firms will at least bring him in to take a look. I was told by many firms that, 'We're not necessarily looking to hire, but why don't you come in and chat.' When I got the offer for my current position I was actively interviewing with a number of other firms.

Venture is very binary—either you make money for the firm, or you don't. I'm here now, and if I show the aptitude to discover good deals and make the firm money then I can probably stay on. If I show an inability to make money, why would they ask me to stick around and why would I want to stay in VC?"

VENTURE CAPITAL

CASE STUDY 25
A Traditional Pre-MBA VC Hire
(see Resume 14)

This person leveraged his consulting experience and electrical engineering degree to land a pre-MBA position.

"I graduated from a school in the Midwest with a degree in electrical engineering. While in school I did two internships—one at IBM and the other at an investment bank where I worked on the tech side supporting the quantitative research group. I decided I didn't want to go into engineering full-time. I liked technology, but I wanted to understand the bigger picture so I decided to go into consulting.

Although my school was not preferred for recruiting, I was able to land an Associate Consultant position at a major firm. I gained wide exposure to companies in the consumer products, automotive and industrial sectors. I ended up getting very little exposure to tech companies. This was a two-year program with an option to stay a third year. Instead of pursuing a third year I decided to target private equity and venture funds. I looked at tech-focused buyout funds and smaller, mid-sized buyout funds. Unfortunately, the initial feedback I got from both PE and VC firms was not encouraging. PE firms told me I didn't have the finance background or deal experience they wanted. The VCs liked my electrical engineering background, but worried that I hadn't been on a consulting engagement with a tech client. I ended up getting dinged by three VC funds and four buyout funds. I did get one offer with a buyout fund, but it was in a city in which I wasn't interested in living.

> *"You should understand your motivations. If you want to be a Partner in venture you should be aware that very few Partners came through the Associate program. There may still be time for you to get into VC later on."*

I eventually clicked with one venture fund that looked past my lack of tech experience. This firm appreciated the fact that I had kept my electrical engineering knowledge up to date. Since the analysis done by a venture fund is more qualitative compared to that done by PE funds, this fund appreciated my consulting background. I was also able to show that the skills I developed in my consulting program would be relevant to the type of venture diligence done at VC funds. I found a venture fund that has less of a desire for Associates to have deep technology experience in the area in which the fund focuses. They looked more for generalists.

Even though I succeeded in securing a VC job, my search was anything but easy. I started with a long list of VC firms and at the end of the day had one offer. I would definitely advise those looking to do their homework. I ended up applying to some firms to which, in retrospect, I would not have applied or at which I would not have wanted to work. I would also tell people to prepare well for interviews. There was a stark difference between the interviews at buyout and VC funds. The buyout Partners grilled me on financial matters, asking me the different ways that I might structure a deal, what different sources of funding I might use and when I would use one over the other. VCs asked more goal-type questions than skill-testing questions. I was asked why I wanted to be an investor. What stage of investing do you like? What types of companies do you like? I know one venture fund that gave candidates an assignment to evaluate a company by coming back with a PowerPoint presentation and model. That seemed a little cumbersome and excessive for an interview process.

VENTURE CAPITAL

Looking back, I should have done more due diligence on firms. I still can't believe that I didn't do more primary research on the funds to which I applied. The venture community is a small one, so there is a lot to be learned about a fund by talking to people in the industry and with people at venture-backed companies even if they didn't get funding from the firm. You should understand your motivations. If you want to be a Partner in venture you should be aware that very few Partners came through the Associate program. There may still be time for you to get into VC later on. If you really want to do operational stuff early on in your career then you can do that and not hurt your chances of getting into VC. You must also be comfortable with the Partners at your firm as you will likely be spending a lot of working time with them.

CASE STUDY 26
A Consultant With A Law Degree Gets In
(see Resume 15)

This candidate went to a top Ivy League school, got a law degree, went into consulting and then made the improbable jump into a healthcare/biotech venture capital fund.

"I came out of undergrad with a double major in Philosophy and Economics and went straight to an Ivy League law school. I didn't have any grand plans. I just wanted to do something intellectually stimulating. While at law school I cross-registered and took some courses at the business school. I passed the New York Bar exam, but went into consulting instead of practicing law. My full-time Associate position at a major consulting shop gave me my first real exposure to business. Although I started as a generalist, I gravitated to pharmaceuticals and biotech and found it more appealing to work with entrepreneurs than with big business.

"I am now the only person at my firm with a JD. I think I brought a different way of thinking to the firm that they liked. So, in my case, I was a good fit and the diversity was a plus. Would it have been better if I had operational experience? Sure!"

I began to look at venture after two years of consulting and it was definitely not an easy jump to make. I used a recruiter who made no promises to me given my background. I knew it would be hard to do so I didn't get my hopes up. I could think of 100 reasons why I should not try to get in, but my thought was, you have to throw your hat in the ring because if you don't you will never get in. Luckily for me I clicked instantly with the fund at which I am now working. They were open-minded about me and took the approach that they would look for talented people who they could train. Since there are so many skill sets needed to do well in venture, firms don't have to take a cookie-cutter approach when hiring. I am now the only person at my firm with a JD. I think I brought a different way of thinking to the firm that they liked. So, in my case, I was a good fit and the diversity was a plus. Would it have been better if I had operational experience? Sure!

Getting a job in venture is dependent on a person's opportunities and, unfortunately, the opportunities don't come around very often. My advice to others would therefore be that they should be proactive and opportunistic. You can't set a plan and say you will follow a certain path and have a job in VC in three years. It doesn't work that way. You must find experiences that will help you reach your goal. Operations experience is, of course, very helpful. Looking back, I may have taken more finance and science classes, but they are not essential. If you are quick and sharp you can learn the ropes. The most important thing is to be passionate about venture investing. You should not be in it for the money and should definitely not come off as if you are. If you are passionate, curious and excited then you will want to learn the science and finance. And, the passion should not just be for venture, it should be for venture, biotech (in my case) and being an entrepreneur."

CASE STUDY 27
Nine Years Of Operating Experience

This person got into venture capital investing with three years of product marketing and six years of engineering experience. He has deep industry knowledge and was at a start-up that successfully went public. He has been at his current VC fund since 2001 and has been promoted twice, but he still says there are no guarantees he will stay on.

"I knew in my mind I was on a technical track and wanted to stay on it when I got my undergrad degree in electrical engineering and followed that with a Masters. I was in no way thinking about venture capital. I can honestly say I didn't even know what venture capital was at that time. Rather, I took a technical position as a design engineer at a technology company. I left that after one year and joined another company, also as a design engineer. I later joined a third company, a start-up communications company, in a similar capacity. It was at this company that I had my first introduction to venture capital.

A couple of weeks after I joined (I was one of the first 15 people at the company) the CEO called everyone into the main conference room and passed around an $8 million check from a VC fund that was our Series B financing. I remember thinking at the time, 'Hey, what's this role of a venture capitalist and how does one become a VC? How do they decide what is a promising opportunity and what isn't? Sometime after that meeting I began to look into the backgrounds of the people at some of the major VC funds and saw a lot of people with Stanford and Harvard MBAs and was intrigued by the fact that there were people solving interesting problems on the business side of the world like I had solved on the

"There were definitely no promises one way or another. I was certainly hoping that I would be on the Partner track. I was told to work hard and prove myself, but there are no guarantees. Nevertheless, I thought that joining the fund would create more options for me even if I were to leave after a few years."

technical side. So, I thought if I ever wanted to do venture I would need to balance my technical knowledge with some business acumen. As I was looking into getting an MBA I also switched over to the business side at my company in product marketing. During my time at this company I saw it go from fewer than 15 people to 600 employees. I saw it get additional funding and was there when it went public. My thoughts were to get into business school and then try and get into venture. If I didn't get into a VC fund I thought I could at least get a senior executive position at a venture-backed start-up.

I applied to business school, but didn't get into Stanford or Harvard. In parallel, I contacted a recruiter that was looking to place Associates at VC firms and said he knew of a VC fund that was looking for someone with my background. The interview process took about six months and the firm seemed in no hurry to bring someone on. I met with everyone on the investment team and was asked things like: What did you learn while at the start-up? What areas do you think are promising to invest in? How would you evaluate investment opportunities? There were no tests or case studies.

I started working at the fund in 2001 and am still there. When I joined, the length of my stay was left open. I was told something like, 'You could just not work out,' 'You could stay a couple of years and leave,' or it was left open that I could stay longer. There were definitely no promises one way or another. I was certainly hoping that I would be on the Partner track. I was told to work hard and prove myself, but there are no guarantees. Nevertheless, I thought that joining the fund would create more options for me even if I were to leave after a few years. I clearly thought that if nothing else I would be exposed to and evaluate numerous business opportunities and enhance my network by meeting the crème-de-la-crème of management teams. I also knew that I would be better equipped to start my own company after the VC experience, and it has certainly worked out that way. I've been promoted twice, first to VP and then to Managing Director. The indications I've gotten are that I'm doing a great job, but I also know that I have to continually perform to stay around—that means sourcing, building and exiting opportunities that create value for our limited partners.

In my case I think the nine years of operating experience I had prior to joining the firm helped and are a significant reason why I am not being told to get more operating experience. If I had to give advice to someone who wanted to get into venture investing, I would first tell them that there is no single path. Every firm is different; some are run by ex-entrepreneurs, some by ex-investment bankers and others by ex-consultants. An MBA from a top school definitely helps, but I think operating experience at a successful start-up is really the critical ingredient. Relevant industry expertise is also important. If you have sector-specific knowledge in a hot industry, when the VC industry stumbles upon it you will be in good shape—just like people who knew optics or telecom in 1999-2000. Basically, I wouldn't worry about whether you will be on the Partner track or not. If you can join for even a few years and see how people build companies, why not do it?"

JOB SPECIFICATIONS

To get a better understanding of what venture capital funds look for when they hire we suggest you take a good look at the job specifications for the following seven positions. Pay careful attention to the description of the roles, the amount of experience sought and the academic and professional training required. Job Searches 1-3 are for pre-MBA positions while Searches 4-7 are for post-MBA roles. You will see that there are usually consistent themes in the requirements for both positions. Both usually require an engineering background, technology expertise, strong academic and professional background and solid research and communications skills, among others. The VC funds are also very clear about whether a job is potentially Partner track (most are not, but some, such as Searches 5 and 7 leave the door open).

Pre-MBA Job Searches

Search 1 | PRE-MBA ASSOCIATE

This is a search for people with 2-5 years experience only (people with more than five years experience were discouraged from expressing interest).

RESPONSIBILITIES
- Pre-qualification of investment opportunities.
- Proactively source new investment opportunities.
- Create competitive landscapes in the Firm's areas of interest.
- Perform research to determine emerging markets within the Firm's areas of investment focus.
- Work with the partners to perform due diligence on potential investment opportunities.
- Work with portfolio companies in all aspects of the company building process.

REQUIREMENTS:
- Minimum of 2-4 years experience at a top-tier management consulting firm, investment bank, or equivalent operating positions.
- Passion and understanding for media, entertainment, and technology industries.
- Understanding of capitalization structures, cap tables, financial analysis, and term sheets.
- Mature personality who can interact with C-level executives.
- Personable, self-motivated, and analytical individual who enjoys operating in an entrepreneurial environment.

Search 2 | PRE-MBA ASSOCIATE

Note the distinct requirement for technology expertise and preference for an engineering degree. This firm specifically defines the time horizon of the role.

REQUIREMENTS:

The Associate candidate will have 2-3 years of experience coming from a top-tier background in strategy consulting, technology operations (technology business, business development or corporate development) or investment banking.

- Must have strong general technology understanding, having worked on several projects in the tech sector; engineering degree is preferred but not required

- Must be ranked at the top of your class with regards to problem solving and quantitative skills

- Must have an extremely high level of maturity and ability to multi-task with little supervision (will not be part of a large group of Associates)

- Must have excellent communication skills both written and oral

- Must have a top academic pedigree (both undergraduate school and GPA)

RESPONSIBILITIES

The Associate role has a broad range of responsibilities, which include:

- Due diligence & investment execution
- Portfolio analysis & fund management
- Consultative projects for existing portfolio companies
- Research into new investment areas

This is a 2-3 year Associate program.

Search 3 | PRE-MBA ANALYST

This fund clearly explains the research and deal support nature of this role, the need to understand the markets in which the fund invests and the importance of working with its portfolio companies.

POSITION DETAILS:

The Analyst will work alongside senior investment professionals to support all aspects of investment evaluation and execution including:

- Original research on market sectors, companies, products and technologies
- Analysis including technical analysis of software architectures and suitability of products for markets
- Financial modeling (valuations, company analysis)
- Participate in firm deal flow sourcing and evaluation
- General due diligence (customer, management checks)
- Assist in transaction processes, deal structuring and deal documentation
- Work with portfolio companies as needed

The ideal candidate will demonstrate ability to conduct original research and assess technology market opportunities, have mature thinking and instinctive good business judgment. The candidate should also have knowledge of at least some market sectors within infrastructure software, applications software, and media and information businesses. The Analyst will be assigned to deal teams and will have the opportunity to take on increasing responsibility within the deal team as he or she demonstrates capability.

REQUIREMENTS:

Candidates for the Analyst role will have demonstrated the ability to rapidly understand and evaluate markets, companies and technologies. Specific requirements include:

- 1 to 3 years of experience in a top-tier management or strategy consulting firm with experience in strategic market analysis; similar strategic analysis experience in a comparable position such as venture or private equity will be considered
- BA/BS from top-tier undergraduate program with superior academic record

IN ADDITION TO:

- Demonstrated knowledge of or strong interest in at least some of the markets where the fund invests: software and information services.
- Demonstrated quantitative and qualitative analysis skills and talent for understanding the evolution of new market segments
- Strong communication and presentation skills, both oral and written.
- Self-starter and a leader with the drive and creativity to find information from multiple sources and the ability to motivate others within a small, rapidly growing firm.
- Ability to build good personal relationships and work closely and credibly with the firm's partners and portfolio companies.

VENTURE CAPITAL

Search 4 | VENTURE ASSOCIATE POSITION (POST-MBA/GRAD SCHOOL LEVEL)

Note the additional (and more detailed) experience required, even though this is still considered a two-year position.

COMPANY:

This established, highly successful Venture Capital firm has a deep history of identifying and investing in disruptive technologies and has performed in the top tier in its peer group over their past several funds.

The post-graduate school level Associate will have 4-8 years of technology-related work experience. The Associate will focus primarily on investments in the consumer wireless space. The Firm is very lean and therefore the Associate will spend the majority of his or her time working directly with the Senior Partners. The expectation is for the position to be a 2-year apprenticeship in Venture Capital.

CANDIDATE REQUIREMENTS:

- Must have a deep understanding of technology, preferably in one of the domain areas listed above.

- Computer Science or Electrical Engineering degree strongly preferred, but technical acumen/background an acceptable substitute.

- Must have a strong complimentary business skill set. Experience at top professional services firm, preferably consulting (even if just for summer though 2 years preferable).

- Should have experience at a high-technology company, preferably in a non-technology/developer role. Preference for candidates with backgrounds in Product Management / Sales /Marketing / Business Development.

- Must be a self-starter, have a high-level of maturity and have superior communication skills. Hard working, outgoing and other strong personal attributes. Part of the role will be to identify and source new business for the firm – a sales background would be a plus.

- Undergrad degree from top school ("Ivy or equivalent") with strong academic performance. Advanced degree, preferably an MBA, from a top school.

VENTURE CAPITAL

Search 5 | POST-GRADUATE LEVEL ASSOCIATE POSITION

This is a healthcare fund; note the specific requirements for a science degree and consulting background with a preference for healthcare experience.

CANDIDATE BACKGROUND:

1 Must have consulting experience. The ideal candidate for this position should have 2-4 years (post grad) experience in the healthcare (particularly biopharma) industry at a top-tier strategy/management consulting firm (McKinsey, Bain, and BCG).

2 Must have a post-graduate school degree (MBA, PhD, MD preferred).

ROLES/REQUIREMENTS:

1 Member of the VC's BioPharma team.

2 Focus on all aspects of due diligence on healthcare opportunities:
   - Locate and interview key physicians
   - Primary and secondary market research
   - Work closely with all members of the biopharma team
   - Good at working out ways to answer difficult questions
   - Highly comfortable with building complex EXCEL spreadsheets

3 Ability to interact effectively with senior management/board members at portfolio companies and potential investments

4 Excellent communication and problem solving skills

5 Sound judgment, based on real world experience, regarding issues faced as the firm does due diligence on companies (e.g. Physician adoption; Technical development issues/intellectual property; Market size; Go-to-market strategies; Regulatory/reimbursement risks; Management team evaluation; Highly self-directed and hard working)

CAREER TRACK:

This opportunity is for a minimum of a 2-year commitment with an opportunity for career retention based on Associate performance and the firm's needs.

| VENTURE CAPITAL |

Search 6 | POST-MBA ASSOCIATE

This VC firm seeks someone with operations experience for a two-year minimum position that very clearly is not Partner track.

The Senior Associate position is NOT intended to be a Partner track position. Candidates are expected to have a high level of maturity, strong presentation skills and a deep network of high-end Entrepreneurs and Venture Capitalists in the area in which the fund is based.

The ideal candidate will have the following:

1 4-7 years of total work experience in technology and network infrastructure/enterprise technology domain experience primarily with an operating company.

2 Ideal backgrounds will include candidates, who have served in Sales and/or Marketing as a Product Line Manager or equivalent position at a technology operating company. We are also open to seeing candidates with previous VC (early and/or late stage) or financial deal experience with technology companies from an investment bank or consulting firm.

3 Solid understanding of technology at the macro and micro levels.

4 Must have exceptional communication skills and a high-level of maturity.

5 Technology due diligence and strong research skills are a top priority.

6 Must have a proactive attitude with good business judgment.

7 Exceptional modeling skills and must be quantitative and analytical.

8 MBA from top school is preferred.

Search 7 | VICE PRESIDENT

This is a Partner-track position and therefore requires many more years of work experience and, preferably, previous venture experience. Candidates are expected to have been significant value creators and have ideally seen a company go through several stages of growth.

VP for Software/Services/Communications Services or Hardware team who would be cultivated throughout the next fund in hopes of achieving a Partner-level promotion within the next 5+ years.

GENERAL PREFERENCES/REQUIREMENTS FOR VP CANDIDATES:

To be considered the VP candidate must have an extensive record of high achievement in their previous endeavors which should span a range of 10-15 years of relevant operating and/or investing experience in Software/Services/Communications Services or Hardware focused industries and preferably at least 3 of those years should be in a venture capital firm or venture backed company. Ideal candidates will have been significant "ring leaders" in their organizations having been an integral contributor to the growth and prosperity of their product groups and/or companies/portfolio companies over an extended period of time. Relevant candidates are expected to be able to cite distinct examples of longer-term value-creation they were responsible for and most likely would have been promoted aggressively as a result (through significant contributions related to Product Management, Marketing, Sales, Engineering, etc.). Preferred candidates would have also been involved with a company throughout several stages of their growth cycle starting from a pre-profit/pre-IPO level progressing towards an IPO/or other liquidity event, and having run larger teams in a multi-faceted, multi-product organization.

A desired profile for this role will be of a candidate who has most likely spent a significant portion of their career in varying operating roles across a few very successful companies augmented with a few years of quality VC investing (where a more intense level of scrutiny will be applied in relation to individual track records and expectations).

For a Hardware candidate, an engineering background is required, with a strong preference for advanced degrees in engineering and/or business (MA, MBA, PhD, etc.).

For a Software/Services/Communications Services candidate, an undergraduate engineering background is preferred (but not required) along with an advanced degree (including an MBA).

The VP candidates will within a few years be expected to lead their own investments and grow into significant Board Level contributors and therefore, on top of strong analytical skills, candidates must be strong communicators, have a high-level of maturity, and exceptional investment judgment.

VENTURE CAPITAL |

chapter IX

Finding The Right Fit

You might think you're ready to work at a private equity fund, but there's probably more you can do to create your best chance of success. Even if you have first-rate finance and deal/project skills you could still end up continually getting turned down for positions, pulling yourself out of contention for others or left with offers that may not be appropriate for you. And, in each case the common denominator is "fit" or more specifically, the lack thereof. In this chapter we will give you some of our guidance on how fit relates to your job search and how finding the best fit can be a springboard to a flourishing career.

If you've been reading this guide closely you will have noticed several mentions of "fit." Maybe you came across these observations: "To me, it is very important that a candidate fit in with the personality of my firm (Insider Tip, Chapter IV)" and "Strategy-wise, I believe it's important to target the right funds given your background. You shouldn't waste your time or the funds' time looking at places where there will not be a good fit (Case Study 14)." What exactly, you may ask, is "fit" and why is it so important to your search? You may think getting a job is all about skills, but it's more than that. It's about finding a place where your skills *and* your personality match what the hiring firm seeks. And, as you can see from the two quotes above, fit is just as important to hiring firms as it is to candidates. We felt the need to advise you on fit because we don't want you to go down the wrong path and miss out on a good opportunity.

Glocap Insight

To find the right PE position it is important to do a thorough self-assessment—what are your interests? What drives you? What are your strengths and weaknesses? What does your experience position you well to do? And, what are your long-term plans? The answers to those questions will serve as a guide for where you want to focus your efforts.

Broken down into its simplest form, selecting a PE fund is a process analogous to selecting a college. That process had two main phases: first you researched and applied to schools and second, after you were accepted, you had to choose one to attend. We believe those phases can serve as a model for how you should go about selecting a PE fund that meshes with your skills and interests. First, we will discuss *Targeting The Right Funds*, which will help kick start the process of analyzing fit for those people just beginning their search. Once you have offers, the next section, *Evaluating Your Choices*, will help you narrow your options so you can pick the place where you are most likely to thrive.

Targeting The Right Funds

SELF ASSESSMENT

For those beginning their search for a position in PE we recommend starting off by conducting a self-assessment to help come up with a potential group of PE funds where you think you will fit in best. The first part of this exercise will help you determine what your skill set includes and what your strengths and weaknesses are. This will narrow down what firms could have interest in you. Once you narrow down which places will be receptive to you, you'll be in a better position to make an intelligent decision about where to interview. As part of this task you should be asking yourself questions such as:

- Am I good at financial modeling?
- Do I have specific industry expertise?
- Do I have hands on exposure to operations?
- Do I think strategically?
- Am I very research intensive?

With the answers to those questions in hand you should turn your attention to the different types of funds that you *want* to pursue. From what we've seen over the years, there are several variables that are important to assess to help narrow the field. These include:

- The investment approach of the fund—some funds work very hands on with their portfolio companies, others are more execution intensive
- The stage of investing—by now you should know that working at a VC fund is very different than working at a later-stage growth fund and/or a buyout fund
- Whether a fund is industry-focused or more of a generalist fund
- The size of the deals and the deal team
- Geography
- Compensation

After a brief look at these variables you should be able to eliminate some additional funds (or at least types of funds). For example, if you know you don't want to do healthcare investments or can't see yourself living in Texas, don't consider firms in either of these categories. Or, if you can't ever see yourself at a five-person, $100 million fund, you will be doing yourself (and a recruiter) a favor by removing that firm from consideration. If there are some funds that you are unsure about you can do further analysis and eliminate some more, but we would recommend not over thinking which ones you will knock off your list at this point. The time to dig deeper is when you have offers on the table, and we will go through a more thorough evaluation of how to do that in the second section when your diligence will be more intense. However, having a manageable list is important as it will allow you to conserve your energy and stay focused and that will ultimately allow you to perform better in your interviews. Otherwise, you may find yourself trying to convince a healthcare VC fund one day that you want to work there, a real estate buyout fund the next and then a general growth equity one, and at the end of the day you will have a tough time sounding persuasive to any of them.

> "I would advise that when targeting PE funds, people should target a narrow subset of funds in which they fit. Taking a shotgun approach will not work."
> – Case Study 8

THE RIGHT FIT

Evaluating Your Choices

If you have one or more offers in hand it's time to embark on deeper diligence to find your perfect match. Where you take your first role, for better or worse, does set your career in motion (just like the college you went to and the first job you took out of school) and therefore we recommend you take the time to choose a place that you truly believe will offer you the best experience.

Going back to the example of when you applied to college, the first part of that search may have led you to target three small liberal arts schools in rural New England, two large universities in the Mid-West and two engineering schools in big cities on either coast. These were all varied institutions, but you had a sincere interest in each of them when you applied. When you were accepted to some of them you had to weigh all the variables, not just the size of schools and geographic location. Given that it was such an important decision, you probably did a thorough evaluation to get a grasp of which school would be the optimal fit for you and thereby help you best get where you wanted to go. You might have talked to alumni and current students and looked into the professors, the academic departments, the sports programs and the overall culture of the student body to help you choose which school to attend. Wouldn't it be smart to put the same effort into deciding which PE offers to accept?

Glocap Insight

There is usually no right or wrong answers when it comes to fit. For example, as it pertains to selecting a college, some people simply prefer big city schools while others like a rural campus. Each have trade-offs, but neither is necessarily better or worse than the other. Beyond analyzing the trade-offs, there is no magic formula to help you choose the place (be it a school or a PE fund) where you will fit best.

In private equity there is a common set of factors that everyone has to consider but candidates prioritize them in different ways. To help you make a choice we will go into more detail about some of the variables we mentioned in Section I and give you the pros and cons of each. It will then be up to you to rank them according to your personality/preferences. When candidates come to us with a choice to make, we advise them to take a step back and ask themselves, "Where do I want to be in five, 10, 15 years? And, which path will be the best step to get me there (or at least leave me with the most options). Indeed, many funds may ask you this as well.

Fit is always important, but it gets more important the more senior you become. For example, if you are finishing business school and are deciding which offer to accept you are making what could be a career decision so you should think even more about fit than pre-MBAs who generally have windows of natural transition ahead of them. That's because whereas earlier in your career you were still *thinking* about your 10-year plan, once you have your MBA it's time to start *implementing* it.

WHAT IS THE FUND'S REPUTATION

Before we get into the different fund variables, we recommend all candidates look out for some universal warning signs. In general most funds that you will come across are legitimate and doing well, however, because we've seen enough examples of people getting into situations that are less than they bargained for we feel the need to alert you to some potential problems. A fund that has a bad reputation and is falling apart is obviously one that should be avoided, but that's an extreme case. Two more frequent signals to look out for are if a firm has had fundraising troubles and if senior professionals have recently left the firm (this could have happened while you were interviewing or right before and you wouldn't have known unless you were plugged in). In fact, any time people have left a fund for reasons other than the natural end of their commitments should at least raise some concern. If you come across a fund with these signs you should do some extra research. Why did the senior people leave? Were they squeezed out? Why is fundraising slow? There could be a legitimate reason and if there is you should find out what it was. On the flip side, if a firm has raised new money and has had a great retention rate, you should probably have little to worry about.

One of the best ways to research the reputation of a fund is to speak with current Associates at the firm or those who used to work there. We have found that those Associates who are rotating out into business school are especially helpful and are usually candid about their experiences. They may also have a handle on other firms, so don't limit your questions to where they worked. We suggest you also take a look at the business schools they are going to as that reflects on the reputation of the fund—are they the same ones in which you would be interested? It's always a good idea to check the industry publications to see if the firm has been in the news lately. If you can't find out about a firm's reputation from people who had worked there other good people to turn to for insight into how a fund is perceived by the PE community could be an investor in PE (like a fund of funds or endowment), a banker that covers PE (financial sponsors) or even a recruiter—for many strong candidates we are happy to (and do) give advice even if we didn't ultimately help them get a job.

IS THE FUND DOING DEALS?

What's the stage of the fund

Clearly, the best place for you to grow and enhance your skills would be at a fund that is actively closing transactions. Before accepting an offer make sure you know when the investment period for the current fund runs out (funds typically have five to six years to deploy capital and usually 10 to 12 years to harvest it), how many deals on average the fund closes, how much uninvested capital ("dry powder") a fund has and if any attempts have been made to raise new money. Then do a careful comparison of the funds at which you have offers. Maybe you're choosing between two well known $1 billion funds. One is four years old and has about $100 million left to invest and the other just raised its fund. Joining the older fund may not give you as much exposure to new deals. Any new deals may be add-ons to existing investments and chances are you could spend a lot of time working with those portfolio companies as well as raising money for the next fund—either can be worthwhile, but may not be what you signed up for. At the newer fund you would probably mostly work on new deals, which may be what you had in mind. We've gotten calls from people looking to make a lateral move out of a firm where fundraising has stalled because they don't want to get stale not doing deals for three years. Taking the right measures now could help you avoid the same situation.

FUND PERFORMANCE

A fund's performance is important both in an absolute sense and vis-à-vis its peer group (for example, funds of the same vintage year). A fund that has consistently performed well will have an easier time attracting new investors than poorer performing or start-up funds. Nevertheless, look into why it performed well. Was it one amazingly successful investment, or several? What are the chances that it will continue to perform well? Are the same people around who made it successful? You may like the idea of joining a start-up fund, but do you have the appropriate risk tolerance? Since there is no fund performance to look at you should focus on the track records of the senior people. It is their reputation that will carry the fund.

INVESTMENT APPROACH

The investment approaches of funds can run the gamut. Some focus on achieving value by finding a good deal at a good price and therefore concentrate on the financial and structuring aspects. Others look to add value post-investment and concentrate on the operational aspects of companies. Most funds would probably say they do both, but since the ball is in your court we recommend you look into what you prefer and where you like to be in that spectrum. Do you enjoy diving into numbers and modeling complex deals? If so, you might want to join a fund that will continue to enhance those skills. Maybe you prefer a more active role with portfolio companies. You can sometimes get a good indication about a fund's investment approach by looking at the backgrounds of the investment professionals. Some funds are loaded with ex-consultants or people with operations backgrounds and will therefore tend to be more hands on, while others that have more former bankers tend to be more focused on the financial aspects of deals.

STAGE

The previous chapters went over the skills required by early-stage venture capital, later-stage growth equity, and leveraged buyout funds (for a refresher take a look at Chapter I). As someone with multiple offers in hand you should be curious if one of those is from a fund that says it invests in companies at more than one stage. In such a situation you should get a better understanding of the target allocation to the various investment stages. This will help you define what you really will be doing. For example, you may want to do extra research on any fund that does some growth equity along with LBOs. Growth equity can involve more deal sourcing and if that is a primary part of the job, but you wanted the LBO deal experience, you may not be right for this fund and vice versa. Either type of fund can offer a great career track platform and there are top firms in each category. You need to figure out what opportunity fits best with what you want to get out of it for the long term.

INDUSTRY FOCUS

Industries come in and out of vogue. The choice you have to make is whether to target an industry-specific or a generalist fund. When considering industry focus you need to think about the pros and cons of specialization. If you become specialized in one industry you will be attractive to some funds, but less so to others. In our experience, focusing on a specific industry can make it tough to diversify into new areas (in Chapter V we pointed out that post-MBAs have a tough time switching industries), but it can be helpful when trying to get an edge. You may have more options if you are a generalist, but may find it difficult to join an industry-specific fund later on. We have seen people succeed choosing either path, but you should at least be aware of the implications of each option.

DEAL SIZE/DEAL TEAM

Both the size of the deals that a fund does and the size of its deal teams are generally dictated by the overall size of the fund. As you would expect, the general rule of thumb is larger funds do bigger deals and have bigger deal teams, while smaller funds usually do smaller deals with smaller deal teams. There are tradeoffs to each. There are more layers of people working on larger deals, but then again, even as a member of an eight-person team, you would be getting exposed to complex transactions with a lot of moving parts and that in itself would be a unique learning experience. You may, for example, play a role in a $10 billion LBO of a company with 10,000 employees spread across 20 divisions in six countries. The deal could have five different capital tranches and a complex set of ownership to evaluate. Even simply being a part of this experience could result in tremendous learning. However, if you are working on a large deal you will likely have less access to portfolio companies and their top management and may have less interaction with senior investment professionals at your firm. Since the larger deals are often done as club deals with other major LBO funds, you could find yourself working with four other LBO shops and have responsibility for only a fraction of the deal. Therefore, while you would be involved in a mammoth deal you should question how much you would be learning and from whom.

Generally, smaller deals are less complex and have fewer moving parts. In a smaller deal you won't come across $2.5 billion debt facilities (a $50 million equity investment with a $30 million mezzanine piece would be more likely). However, the smaller deal teams (it could be just you and one other person) can mean more responsibility in executing the investment, more involvement with portfolio companies and the senior management of your fund. You could even be traveling with a Partner and dealing with the CEO of a company when the Partner can't and therefore learning how to run a business as well.

As with the other variables discussed in this chapter, there are no right or wrong answers. You must decide which place will be the best experience for you. If the size of the deals and deal teams are similar you might want to go to the fund with the leaner teams. Such a situation could occur if you have offers from two $1 billion funds that do control buyouts and have performed well. Thinking about the size of the fund that you enjoy is also important because firms may begin labeling you as a small fund person or a big fund person depending on where you work. This will come into play if you decide to make a lateral move down the road. Keep in mind that there is general bias toward hiring people to do the same size deals that they have done in the past, though historically, it has been more common for investors to move from doing bigger deals to smaller ones rather than the reverse.

GEOGRAPHY

Geographic preference is more than picking a fund in a city where you want to live. Of course, you shouldn't go to a fund that is in a city where you don't want to be. But you should also not assume that one fund is better than another because of its physical location. There are definitely $500 million funds in smaller cities that are more reputable than $500 million ones in major financial centers. If you join a reputable firm in a smaller city you will still be marketable to funds in other cities later on.

We've been asked by candidates with multiple offers if they should take what they think is an A- opportunity in a major city or an A+ one in a smaller locale. If you are truly open to any geography, we will stick to our theme that you should go after the best learning experience and therefore shouldn't let where you will live get in the way. You should look carefully at the brand, the people and the reputation of the funds where you have offers. Even if your friends haven't heard of a specific fund, if top caliber people are there industry pros should be aware of the fund.

COMPENSATION

How you are compensated naturally plays some role in whether you accept a position, but we continue to stress that finding the best place to advance your career should be as important as the money that you will make. The idea is that finding the best platform will give you the best prospects for long-term compensation. We like it when people tell us they want to be compensated fairly and that they seek an environment where they will be learning the most. These are the candidates who tend to realize that being somewhere that will teach and develop them can be the best compensation. If you can get paid a lot and learn a lot then you've found a good place. Alternatively, it may not be worth it if you end up at a firm where you are earning a lot, but may be sacrificing learning. Some candidates can probably afford to take a risk and go to a start-up fund that is being run by top people even if at the beginning it doesn't offer as much cash, but where you can grow and over time receive a percentage of the carried interest (see Chapter XII for a more detailed discussion on carry and compensation).

chapter X

THE RESUME

Preparing a top-notch resume is a necessary but not sufficient requirement to securing a PE job. Recruiters, and in fact most anyone in a hiring position who has looked at hundreds of resumes, are extremely adept at sizing up candidates very quickly based on their resume. This chapter will discuss the role of your resume, give detailed suggestions about what we think should and should not be included and go over our thoughts on the general structure. Following that you will find 15 actual resumes that correspond to the Case Studies that appeared throughout Chapters IV-VIII.

The main function of a resume is to get you in the door. Therefore, in our opinion, your goal when putting together a resume should be to present a thorough and accurate picture of yourself and what you have done with the view toward landing an interview. You should, at all costs, strive to avoid harming yourself by using excessive (and unnecessary) embellishment or over-the-top phrases (see *The Personal Section* below). You are who you are and as long as you present yourself well and stay within the norms of accuracy your resume should serve the purpose you want it to.

We evaluate thousands of candidates each week and look for crisp and clean resumes with an easy-to-read format, simple fonts and *zero* typographical errors. Even one typo, one off-color font or format or excessive language could be reason enough to separate one qualified candidate from another. Some schools—Harvard Business School is one we know of—have figured out the importance of putting together a streamlined resume that presents an easy-to-read summary of a candidate's education and work history. We think this consistent format helps readers focus on the content of the resume without the distraction of different formats.

As recruiters placing people into high-end positions at PE/LBO and venture capital funds, we work off the initial assumption that every resume we see will be at a certain clear, legible, descriptive baseline especially given the caliber of professionals we presume we are dealing with. As we examine it further, the content and extra accomplishments and the way they are presented can either move the candidate up a notch in our mind, or perhaps drop him/her a notch. For example, a candidate will come off as attractive if he/she has a solid academic performance, good work experience and a well thought out clear career progression. That same person will appear even stronger if the academic and work experiences are supplemented with additional achievements and, of course, if those are portrayed well on their resume.

Keeping in mind the main goal of the resume, we want you to maximize your experiences on paper and don't want you to miss out on an interview because you omitted something or worded it poorly. From our perspective, if you have a solid academic and professional background, with a combination of banking, consulting and/or private equity, you should draw some interest as long as you have put together a good resume that reflects that background. It's the others who will have to probably go the extra step to make sure their resume is the best it can be (without lying/embellishing) to perhaps give them a needed leg up to differentiate them in the process. Below are some general suggestions of what we think you probably should and should not include and how best to organize your resume.

BE HONEST

We cannot stress enough that you are who you are and your resume is not a place to pretend you're someone else. That means don't list things you have not done or embellish things that you have. Expect that your resume will be checked and this includes test scores, GPAs, work experiences and athletic accomplishments—some firms ask for transcripts, or graduation degrees, almost all ask for references and will check them. Putting something in that doesn't belong is simply not worth the risk.

IT'S ALL ABOUT DEALS

Highlight and list your deals/projects and be cognizant of the fact that anything you list is fair game to be discussed, so don't list something that you didn't work on or that you are not prepared to talk about. You should break all deals down individually and list your responsibilities along with the size of the deal, the structure used and the status—has the deal closed or is it pending. Since not everyone is familiar with company names you should be clear about the industry in which you have done deals. If you're at a PE fund which is doing deals you should take this one step further and describe your current fund by mentioning its name, size, the stage of deals on which it focuses (can be multiple) and the industry focus if there is one. If you have a lot of deal experience we suggest putting together a separate deal sheet as an addendum to your resume.

ACCOMPLISHMENTS/SPECIAL RESPONSIBILITIES

In addition to listing your work experience, it's important to list any other accomplishments or special responsibilities you have had along the way. Maybe you led a team of Analysts, did some special work for the chairman of your company on an internal project or represented your company overseas. Perhaps you were tapped by upper management to be involved in recruiting or training. In our opinion, any of these could indicate that you were considered a leader and a trusted representative of the firm and it will stand out as added differentiation from our perspective.

AVOID MORE THAN ONE PAGE

We're of the school of thought that a nice crisp resume is always one page, especially for anyone with 10 or less years of work experience. We have seen very senior people squeeze their experiences into one page, so we think you should be able to as well. The exception to this rule is if you have specific additional information—such as a deal sheet, a list of patents you were granted or papers you have published (this is especially true with academics and PhDs). These can be included as part of a supplemental appendix.

DON'T FORGET THE MONTHS

Although some well known guidelines suggest otherwise, we think it's beneficial to always list the month and year you started and ended a position. If you left a job in December 2005, but your resume just says "2005," someone reading your resume in January 2006 will not know if you have been out of work for 10 days, 10 weeks or 10 months.

OBJECTIVES

Not all resumes need to include an objective at the top. If you have a background that is common for the position you are pursuing an objective might be redundant. An objective can be more helpful for someone whose background may seem like a further stretch for the role they want (this may be someone who is changing careers or industries). In such a case an objective should be written explaining why your skills are applicable for the specific position.

COVER LETTERS

Although cover letters usually go hand-in-hand with resumes we don't feel they are always necessary. If you are sending a resume directly to a hiring firm we would recommend including a cover letter. However, if you are working with a recruiter a cover letter is not necessary because most of the recruiter's role is to assess your skills and frequently they will do their own write-up about why you are appropriate for a specific role.

TEST SCORES MATTER

GPAs and test scores are relevant for your entire career. Always list them to at least one decimal point. Some people with high GPAs sell themselves short by not including it because "they heard it does not matter once you are more senior or post B-school." List GMAT and SAT scores if they are good to great. We would recommend holding off if they were very low. For MBAs, business school GPAs are not worth including, but top class distinctions such as a Baker or Arjay Miller Scholar from Harvard Business School or Stanford's Graduate School of Business should be mentioned.

WHAT ABOUT HIGH SCHOOL?

High school information should generally not be included unless it is pretty significant—i.e.: valedictorian of a 500-student graduating class or class president. Some graduates of prep or private schools may list their schools as those ties among alumni seem pretty strong. Listing a major accomplishment/leadership position such as being captain of a varsity team, newspaper editor or member of a championship team is acceptable. But, the listing should be brief.

THE PERSONAL SECTION

Always include a personal section on your resume. This is the one and only area where you can be creative. List some of your true hobbies/interests/accomplishments. Do not try to write ones that you think people want to read—avid crocodile wrestler, drag racer and base jumper—unless you really do those things. Firms and recruiters can see through that and size you up pretty quickly. Golf, hiking, fly fishing, coaching soccer, playing piano, tutoring, photography, ballroom dancing, judo and traveling are all pretty descriptive and neutral. Being a contestant on college Jeopardy or a child actor is also interesting. Wine tasting, reading spy novels, driving the Amalfi Coast, avid Cincinnati Reds fan, are all fine but approaching the limits. Smoking fine cigars while drinking single malt whiskey, playing with my two *beautiful* children, saying you enjoy intellectual political commentary or watching ESPN are probably over the top and could potentially hurt you.

LANGUAGE/INTERNATIONAL

Language skills and dual citizenship may be included in the personal section. However, if you are really pushing for an international career you could list these in a separate section adding levels of proficiency ie: native French speaker, fluent in German and business German, conversational in Mandarin.

SOME OTHER DO'S AND DON'TS

- De-emphasize older, less relevant work experience (i.e., summer jobs unless brand name firms or jobs during college).

- There is never a need to write "references available upon request." In the realm of private equity recruiting it is assumed that you can present several references.

- In the current world of e-mail don't worry too much about paper. In most cases if a resume needs to be printed it will be off of an e-mail. Since recruiters will e-mail your resume on to clients we recommend you make sure the document doesn't have passwords or fancy formatting that can get lost in older versions of software.

- Whatever contact information you include is fair game so make sure what you list (e-mail, mobile phone, work phone, home phone) is in working order and that it is safe for a recruiter or firm to use.

Sample Resumes

On the following pages are a series of 15 resumes of people from varying backgrounds who all got private equity jobs. As indicated at the top of each resume, these correspond to the Case Studies throughout the book. We have slightly altered these per the requests of the people who were gracious enough to allow us to reprint them. We feel the resumes provide a good glimpse of what makes certain candidates attractive to private equity funds because, except for the modifications, the resumes are similar to how they appeared when each candidate landed their PE interviews. Resume 6 is particularly short because this person got into PE directly out of undergrad and didn't have an extensive work history.

We recommend you look at all of the resumes in this section regardless of the level of the candidates or the path they took. But, we suggest you make an extra effort to look for a resume from someone who is at the same entry point as you and compare your resume to theirs, both for style and substance. Also, take a look at what makes each person stand out. Sometimes it's their personal experiences, other times it's their academic or career accomplishments. Either way most were able to sell themselves without using unnecessary embellishment.

When you look at the resumes, focus on how they describe work experiences and what they include in the personal sections. To help you out, each resume has a section at the top called "Recruiter's Perspective" in which we point out the strong points and the items that jump out at recruiters and hiring firms when scanning the resume. Some resumes also have notes under "Pluses." These are not the ubiquitous action words that many resume guides suggest using; rather they are specific achievements that give the candidate added points in the eyes of our recruiters. Rankings of undergraduate institutions on each resume come from U.S. News & World Report's list of America's Best Colleges 2006. The business school rankings are from Business Week's 2004 ranking of best MBA programs (note: this ranking is done every two years).

Resume 1

Profile
Pre-MBA:
Bulge-Bracket On Cycle Hire
(see CASE STUDY 1)

Recruiter's Perspective
- Brand name I-bank
- Top school
- Solid GPA/SAT scores
- Well-rounded (fraternity, club)
- Interacted with senior bankers, clients and lawyers
- Phi Beta Kappa

Pluses

Varsity tennis...3rd in high school class... summa cum laude in college

Work Experience

Bulge Bracket Investment Bank, New York, NY   *July 2004 - Present*

Analyst
- Designed and manipulated integrated financial models to evaluate various financing and acquisition scenarios
- Performed corporate and asset valuation analysis using discounted cash flow, comparable trading, comparable transaction and leveraged buyout methodologies
- Developed financial projections and detailed operating models for clients
- Worked directly with the client in a one-on-one setting in order to properly model assets for potential Master Limited Partnership ("MLP") formation
- Analyzed transactions to determine accretion / dilution impact and credit implications
- Modeled MLP transactions and performed analysis including G.P. valuation, incentive distribution rights ("IDRs") and cash parity under an IDR re-set
- Prepared presentations and marketing materials including board presentations, rating agency presentations, due diligence presentations, roadshow presentations and investor presentations
- Interacted with senior bankers, client management and lawyers on a daily basis

Selected transactions include:
  - ~$160 million IPO
  - $113 million common unit offering
  - $130 million common unit offering
  - $1.1 billion of Series A Notes
  - $230 million common unit offering and $275 million of Senior Notes

Regional Bank, New York, NY   *Summer 2003*

Intern, Public Finance Department
- Built a comprehensive database of debt issues, issuer credit characteristics, credit enhancement and liquidity facilities
- Analyzed the trading of municipal securities after issue, determined the extent of bank's access to retail accounts through institutional intermediaries, and performed industry research

Boutique Investment Bank, New York, NY   *Spring 2002*

Analyst
- Performed industry research, compiled industry and company overviews, and performed financial research
- Performed valuation analysis, created pitchbooks, analyzed and compiled financials, and composed a memorandum for a debt offering

Education

Top 10 Undergrad   *2000 - 2004*

Bachelor of Arts in Economics, 2004
- Graduated summa cum laude with a GPA of 3.89 and a major GPA of 3.87
- Journalist for independent weekly newspaper
- Phi Beta Kappa Society, Golden Key National Honor Society
- Psi Upsilon Fraternity, Entrepreneur's Club

High School, 1996 - 2000
- Graduated 3rd in class of 400
- SAT: 800 Verbal / 770 Math
- National Merit Scholarship Winner, Advanced Placement Scholar with Distinction
- Member of Varsity Tennis team for four years

Interests

Baseball, Basketball, Golf, Tennis, Skiing, Music, Reading

Resume 2

Profile
Pre-MBA: Getting In From A Consulting Program
(see CASE STUDY 3)

EXPERIENCE

Major Consulting Firm, Analyst — 2002-2004
- *Growth strategy.* Developed a national business growth strategy for a telecom regional bell operating company to achieve an additional $3.5 billion in annual profitability.
- *Market entry strategy.* Formulated a comprehensive enterprise mobility strategy for a Fortune 25 IT services company.
- *Mergers and acquisitions.* Evaluated potential acquisition targets for a leading data storage device company as part of a broader full potential project.

Software Company, Founding Employee and Business Development Manager — 2000-2001
- *Product/market strategy.* Drove product line from concept to execution. Led cross-functional effort to articulate strategy, create collateral, model pricing, and orchestrate sales efforts.
- *Strategic sales and Channel development.* Led sale of $1 million software/services contract. Negotiated strategic channel relationships. Facilitated acquisition of Series B venture financing.
- *Alliance development.* Executed and managed over 20 strategic partnerships with leading technology providers, system integrators, and channel resellers.
- *Team-building.* Ignited early recruiting efforts and helped to drive critical growth as a founding employee.

Media/Broadcasting Company

Production Assistant / Technology Correspondent — Fall 1999
- *Technology reporting.* Spearheaded, wrote, directed, and produced an investigative news package on the emerging technology and Internet sector in Asia.
- *Industry analysis.* Supported anchors and reporters by providing key industry knowledge and insights for their tech-focused stories.
- *Executive interviews.* Led research efforts, developed questions, and participated in interviews of luminaries like Microsoft's Steve Ballmer.

Leading Investment Bank, Financial Analyst — Summer 1998
- *Financial modeling.* Modeled profitability and optimized capital structure of a $400 million joint venture in the transportation industry.
- *Capital structure analysis.* Examined financing covenants impacting the capital structure for major telecom company resulting in a $3 billion credit facility.
- *Risk assessment.* Analyzed and modeled critical risk factors and their associated financial impact on a multi-billion dollar offshore oil and gas projects.

EDUCATION
Top Five University

M.S., Engineering — June 2002
- Concentration in Technology Management / Entrepreneurship with relevant coursework, including Strategy in Technology Based Companies, High Tech Marketing, Computer Networks, and Change Management.
- Research Associate
- GPA: 3.97/4.0; GRE: 2210

B.S. with Distinction, Engineering — March 2000
- Executive roles in various student organizations.
- Major GPA: 3.99/4.0; Cumulative GPA: 3.88/4.0

SKILLS / INTERESTS
- Proficient with SQL, Access, C, HTML, and Excel financial modeling.
- Spoken Mandarin Chinese.

Profile
Pre-MBA:
Getting In From A Regional Bank
(see CASE STUDY 4)

Recruiter's Perspective
- Top School
- Top GPA
- Solid leverage experience
- Closed four deals
- Well-rounded (see Varsity Baseball)
- Prime example of top candidate from regional bank

Pluses

Originated, structured and executed loans...Awarded 3rd year offer...Assisted in creation of new LBO model... 4-time varsity letter winner...Two-time conference champion...*Elected captain of baseball team and president of alumni club* (shows peer respect)

Experience

Mid-Market Investment Bank
Financial Analyst, Leveraged Finance Group

- Originated, structured, and executed syndicated loans and high yield transactions for leveraged buy-outs, mergers, acquisitions, and recapitalizations
- Created offering memoranda, management presentations, rating agency presentations, and road show presentations
- Executed internal analysis for senior credit underwriting process, including memoranda for initial screening, commitment committee, and sales force marketing
- Performed detailed historical and projected comparative financial analysis to evaluate company credit quality, industry trends, and capital markets trends
- Awarded 3rd year offer

Selected Transactions:

- Regional Manufacturer
  - Sole lead manager on $100MM senior subordinated note offering to fund $175MM acquisitio
  - Sole lead manager on $150MM senior secured credit facilities to complete recapitalization

- Restaurant Operator
  - Sole lead manager on $200MM senior subordinated note offering to fund $300MM acquisition

- Technology Services Provider
  Sole lead manager on $150MM senior secured credit facilities to complete recapitalization

Education

Ivy League University
B.A. in History,   1998 - 2002
- Awarded university scholarship for academic achievement
- Senior Honors Paper
- 4-time varsity letter winner in baseball

High School   1994 - 1998
- Top 5% in class with 3.9 GPA
- Elected captain of baseball team

Leadership

University Varsity Baseball   1998 – 2002
- Two-time conference champion

Regional Alumni Club   2003 – 2004
- Elected President of 300 member regional alumni club

Investment Bank Training Program – Mid-Market Investment Bank   2003 – 2004
- Assisted in creation of new LBO model for firm's Investment Banking platform
- Developed extensive case study to instruct incoming and future analysts about financial modeling and the execution of the underwriting process

Profile
Pre-MBA: Getting In From A Mid-Market Bank—Late Cycle
(see CASE STUDY 5)

EXPERIENCE

Mid-Market Investment Bank
2003-2005

Financial Analyst – Investment Banking, Corporate Finance Group

This middle market investment bank, providing investment advisory, fairness opinion, solvency opinion, valuation opinion, restructuring advisory, and portfolio management services to over 1,000 clients ranging from closely held companies to Global 500 corporations.

- Performed extensive modeling and quantitative valuation analyses, including leveraged buyout, discounted cash flow, accretion / dilution, and merger analyses; constructed integrated standalone and pro forma financial models. Completed covenant flexibility, borrowing base availability, cash flow, and debt instrument analyses for clients on both financing and M&A transactions
- Conducted due diligence, analyzed potential synergies, and sensitized financial models
- Conducted industry research (market size, market share, industry trends, competitive landscape, customer trends) to both market companies and determine the correct market niche and possible arenas for expansion
- Project experience includes:
  - Advisor on the sale of a large franchisee of a national car rental agency
  - Advisor on an accelerated sale process for a defense electronics company with a preemptive offer by a large conglomerate
  - Engaged by a private equity sponsor for the sale/recapitalization of a courier services business
  - Advisor on the sale of a privately owned defense electronics company
  - Advisor on the sale of a privately owned semiconductor capital equipment company
  - Engaged to raise a senior and subordinated debt for a public apparel company
  - Advisor on the management / equity sponsor buyout and the associated financing of a Las Vegas casino
  - Advisor on the sale of a HVAC / refrigeration company
- Prepared financing and strategic alternatives presentations to clients in a range of industries, including apparel, real estate, and technology
- Ranked as the top analyst in class and received the highest ratings for learning ability and modeling skills

Private Equity Firm
Spring & Summer 2003

Analyst Intern –Generalist Group

This firm is concerned primarily with mezzanine investments in high growth but low technology industries
- Conducted thorough analysis of transactions to analyze returns on specific investments and assess fund performance to-date
- Assisted the Chief Operations Officer in reconciling accounts and past transactions, and identifying potential investment opportunities within the current portfolio
- Completed industry and company analyses within various sectors which included transportation and apparel

Private Equity Firm
Summer & Fall 2002

Summer Analyst Intern

Focuses on special situation investment opportunities within various industries, exclusive of the high technology and telecommunications industries
- Conducted quantitative and qualitative due diligence on public and private companies for the purposes of evaluating potential investment opportunities, authoring comprehensive company and industry analyses
- Conducted extensive research within the paperboard, cosmetics, and specialty chemicals industries
- Created stand-alone LBO and merger models and evaluated various capital structure and financing alternatives on potential investments
- Performed discounted cash flow and accretion / dilution analyses and performed comparable company and M&A transaction analyses
- Prepared information packages and presentations for prospective clients

Venture Capital Fund
Spring 2002

Research Intern

This seed venture capital firm concentrated on investments within the nanotechnology sector
- Researched potential sources of intellectual property within certain accredited universities conducting research in the nanotechnology sector
- Corresponded and evaluated various technology transfer offices to evaluate potential co-investment opportunities

EDUCATION

Top 30 University-School of Business
1999-2003

B.S. degree in Business Administration, Emphasis in Corporate Finance, Magna Cum Laude
- Cumulative GPA: 3.85/4.00; Dean's List: 1999-2003
- Presidential Scholarship for Academic Achievement

High School
1995-1999

SAT-I: 1520 (Verbal: 780; Math: 740)

ACTIVITIES

Fraternity, Ski Club
2000-2002, 1999-2000

Profile

Pre-MBA: An Accountant Gets In—Later in The Cycle

(see CASE STUDY 6)

EXPERIENCE

MAJOR ACCOUNTING FIRM   **NEW YORK, NY**

Associate, Corporate Finance - Transaction Structuring Group

- Advised investment banks, private equity firms, Fortune 500 companies and other corporate clients on the financial accounting and reporting, regulatory aspects and tax implications of complex financial transactions. Involved in the structuring of mergers and acquisitions, off-balance sheet financings, leveraged buyouts/recapitalizations, dispositions, joint ventures, leasing transactions and financial derivative products.

- Worked on site at a client in Europe to assist in the structuring of the sale of a $1.6 billion equity investment in a local telecommunications subsidiary to a Fortune 100 company.

- Spent three months in Asia investigating the events which led to a $2.6 billion loss incurred by a major Asian commodities trading corporation.

- Analyzed business development strategies that would enable a Fortune 100 company to enter a new line of business while achieving desired balance sheet and income statement presentation results.

- Assisted in the structuring of the leveraged recapitalization of a home products corporation that would provide substantial accounting and tax benefits to a large private equity firm.

- Provided a pooling-of-interests analysis for a foreign company on the acquisition of a U.S. corporation.

EDUCATION

1992 – 1996

IVY LEAGUE

Bachelor of Science in Economics. Graduated cum laude with a dual concentration in Finance and Entrepreneurial Management.
Finance/Management GPA: 3.7/4.0, Cumulative GPA: 3.6/4.0.

PERSONAL

Worked over fifteen hours per week for seven semesters to help defray educational costs. Enjoy golf, running, swimming, music and traveling.

Profile
Pre-MBA: Directly Out Of Undergrad—An Exception
(see CASE STUDY 7)

Recruiter's Perspective
- Top GPA
- High GMAT (taken as undergrad)
- Strong internships
- High-energy person (see Skills and Interests)

Pluses
Cold-calling (not afraid of the phone)… Leveraged buyout transactions…4.0 GPA… 740 GMAT… Phi Beta Kappa…Surfer… Rock climber

EXPERIENCE

11/97 – 5/99   **Intern,** Start-Up Tech Company, Palo Alto, CA

Developed marketing strategy for angel-funded 3D graphics software tools startup. Produced marketing materials and company publications. Sold software through cold-calling and trade shows; efforts led to sales to multiple marquee customers.

6/98 – 9/98   **Intern,** Consulting Firm, London, England

Evaluated and drafted recommendations on potential leveraged buyout transactions for a $650 million private equity fund managed by the firm. Conducted interviews of customers, competitors, and industry experts. Performed public company and comparable transaction analyses.

EDUCATION

9/96 – 6/99   **Top Five University**

BA in History (4.0 GPA) with honors and University distinction awarded June 1999. Elected to Phi Beta Kappa. Departmental honors thesis accepted with high honors. GMAT: 740.

3/98 – 6/98   **Overseas University,** England

9/95 – 5/96   **Johns Hopkins University,** Baltimore, MD

SKILLS AND INTERESTS

- Avid surfer, rock climber, and skier
- Elementary German speaker

Resume 7

Profile
Pre-MBA: From Industry
Into A Healthcare Fund
(see CASE STUDY 8)

EXPERIENCE

Major Biotech Company — 2001-2003

Manager, Strategic Planning Group

Responsible for financial and strategic planning for novel cancer therapy product.

- Financial Analysis:
  - Created financial model to forecast future cash flows based on multiple clinical development plans.
  - Performed valuation and sensitivity analysis.
  - Presented financial analysis to senior management.
- Market Research:
  - Led team in quantitative assessment of new markets in order to identify future growth opportunities.
  - Developed US pricing strategy.
  - Identified target physician segments for sales force to call on at launch using primary research.
  - Co-led efforts with brand team to develop global positioning statement and key launch messages.
- Managed MBA summer intern.

Manager, Business Development Group

Promoted to Manager within 17 months of hiring and was the only manager without an MBA or other advanced degree.

- Evaluated market opportunities and built valuation models for over ten business development assessments.
- Managed due diligence process and provided recommendations on whether or not to pursue deals.
- Worked on deal team to in-license development rights for an early stage cancer product.
- Expanded international forecasting capabilities through the development of a global financial model.
- Developed competitive intelligence as a core competency for three other brands.

SOFTWARE COMPANY, San Francisco, CA — 2000-2001

Business Analyst

- Worked in product marketing, corporate development and sales for an early-stage software company. Acquired in fall of 2001.
- Conducted competitive market analysis of 100 private companies in the software/technology sectors.
- Provided strategic recommendations on acquisition targets to the Board of Directors.
- Created new product line and developed branding, pricing structure and client database.
- Received award for sourcing the most sales meetings of all employees through cold calling.

EDUCATION

IVY LEAGUE — 1996-2000

B.A. in Human Biology with Academic Honors
- Courses: Corporate Finance, Accounting, Statistics, Genetics, Immunology, Vaccine Development and Organic Chemistry.

LEADERSHIP ACTIVITIES

VENTURE PHILANTHROPHY FUND, San Francisco, CA — 2001-2003

Engagement Manager
- Led diligence team to identify and invest $50K into two non-profit organizations for this venture philanthropy fund. Provide ongoing strategic and operational support to the fund's grantees.

NON-PROFIT — 1998-2000

Founder and Director
- Founded regional site of national non-profit health care organization, with 300 volunteers, 10 full-time staff and offices in four U.S. cities.

INTERNATIONAL DEVELOPMENT ORGANIZATION — Summer 1999
- Principal Investigator. Directed 10-person field research team to evaluate the sustainability of a regional community health program.

MEDICAL RELIEF ORGANIZATION — Summer 1998
- Emergency Medical Technician. Traveled with 4-person medical team to provide public health infrastructure to remote villages.

ATHLETICS

Captain of semi-pro four-person adventure racing team — 2000-2003
- Earned consistent top-ten finishes in 24-hour, 70+ mile adventure races.

Profile
Pre-MBA:
From Industry To Buyouts
(see CASE STUDY 9)

experience

2001-2003	**Microsoft Corporation**	Redmond, WA

Program Manager / Software Design Engineer

Defined the strategy, design, and implementation of Microsoft's next generation communication and entertainment product.

- **Business and Product Strategy:**
  - Presented product to MS senior executive staff and key industry influentials.
  - Defined core thinking behind brand strategy and long term business plan.
  - Drove product launch in Europe
- **Software Development**
- Led networking infrastructure development for Microsoft's peer-to-peer application.
  - Designed and implemented a distributed a peer-to-peer file system (patented).
  - Filed for 5 patents as inventor.

Summer 2000   **Telecom Company**

Program Manager / Software Engineer

Architected audio content management system; Filed for 2 patents as inventor.

Summer 1999	**Microsoft Corporation**	Redmond, WA

Software Design Engineer

Designed and implemented a core component of the Microsoft consumer operating system.
Ranked in the top decile of Microsoft's interns.

1997-1999   **Online Game Company**

Senior Designer / Founder

Designed and implemented the internet's largest online text based MMOG (60 thousand total users, 500 current users). Led an international team of over 30 developers.

education

1997-2001   **Ivy League University**

Bachelor of Arts degree in Computer Science, Magna Cum Laude. GPA (3.8/4.0)

Interests   Complex systems / machine learning, finance, running, creative writing, electronic music, photography.

Resume 9

Profile
Post-MBA:
Returning To Your Pre-MBA Firm
(see CASE STUDY 10)

Education

2003 - 2005

TOP 5 BUSINESS SCHOOL

Candidate for Master in Business Administration degree, June 2006.

1995 - 1999

TOP 5 UNDERGRAD

Bachelor of Arts with Honors in Economics. Focus on international development.
Women's varsity sport.

Work Experience

summer 2004

MANUFACTURING COMPANY

Operations Intern

- Conceived and executed improvements to address fulfillment of missing, wrong, and damaged parts. Designed and implemented associated company-wide IT modifications, and developed productivity improvement plan with $200,000 annual savings.

2001 - 2003

Top-Tier, Multi-Billion LBO Fund

Evaluated and executed equity and debt investments in the U.S. and Europe for large private equity fund. Developed operating models, restructuring models, and valuation analyses for leveraged buyout and distressed debt investments. Authored and presented investment memos to investment committee.

- Transaction A. Conducted comprehensive business, financial, and industry due diligence. Coordinated legal, accounting, and other advisory teams. Executed $400 million of new high-yield and asset-backed financing. Worked with management to assess potential raw material sourcing strategies and identify near-term follow-on acquisitions.

- Transaction B. Drafted and negotiated transaction documents, financing agreements, and management contracts. Completed bank and high-yield debt refinancing. Worked closely with senior and middle management to determine growth strategies and implementation plans for new products. Developed long term budget, identified acquisition targets, and evaluated strategic partnerships and marketing plans.

- Transaction C. - Evaluated a variety of strategic alternatives for portfolio company, culminating in $2 billion take-private transaction. Executed refinancing of $500 million of senior notes.

1999 - 2001

INVESTMENT BANK-A

Restructuring Analyst (December 2000 - July 2001)
Mergers & Acquisitions Analyst (July 1999 - December 2000)

Summer 1998

INVESTMENT BANK-B

Financial Analyst - Consumer Group

summer 1997

Researcher-Writer - France and Europe Guides

Personal

Fluent in French. Enjoy comedy films, playing sports, and traveling. Citizenship: U.S. and U.K.

Profile
Post-MBA: Returning With Narrow Geographic Preferences
(see CASE STUDY 11)

THE RESUME

education
2004 - 2006 TOP 5 BUSINESS SCHOOL

Candidate for Master in Business Administration degree, June 2006. Recipient of Scholarship for demonstrated leadership and values. Member of VC & Private Equity Club.

1996 - 2000 TOP 25 UNIVERSITY

Bachelor of Business Administration degree, *summa cum laude*, in Finance and Business Economics. Minor in Accountancy. GPA 3.84/4.00.

experience
Summer 2005 ABC CAPITAL GROUP
Investment Analyst

Responsible for evaluating investment opportunities for a $750 million value-oriented hedge fund.

- Analyzed opportunities in consumer products, shipping, media and education through a combination of fundamental analysis, management interviews and industry research.
- Conducted in-depth industry analysis. Recommendations led to several investments.

2002 - 2004 LBO Fund
Private Equity Associate

One of 25 investment professionals managing $6 billion of private equity capital.

- Responsible for transaction execution, structuring investments, financial modeling, conducting due diligence, managing external advisors, securing debt financing, reviewing contracts and recruiting executives.
- Completed $190 million leveraged buyout of Pharmaceutical company. Actively involved in securing the debt financing package, negotiating agreements and conducting extensive due diligence. Closely evaluated products and markets, discovering substantial undeveloped value in key products resulting in over $15 million in incremental EBITDA.
- Identified attractive healthcare segments and networked with potential CEO partners. Proactively pursued investments in generic pharmaceuticals, specialty pharmaceuticals, medical products, hospitals and managed care. Evaluated over 50 healthcare investment opportunities independently and in conjunction with partner-CEOs
- Led six-month proactive industry effort in the Medicare HMO industry. Built relationships with dozens of prominent managed care executives.
- Worked closely with management teams of portfolio companies to review add-on acquisitions and improve business performance.
- Created investment thesis for a consolidation in the active pharmaceutical ingredients industry.
- Actively involved in Associate recruiting. Led recruiting efforts during the 2003-2004 season.

2000 - 2002 Mid-Market Investment Bank
Investment Banking Analyst
- One of 10 M&A investment bankers advising on over $4 billion in transaction volume per year.
- Top ranked analyst in first and second year.
- Advised food company on $700 million acquisition.
- Advised company on its $100 million sale to telecom company. Achieved purchase price 60% higher than originally anticipated.

community
Founded community business association for high school students designed to develop business skills. Activities included mock investing and entrepreneurship projects.

personal
Climbed Mount Kilimanjaro (19,300 feet). Avid basketball player. Enjoy international travel (Europe, Southeast Asia and Africa).

Resume 11

Profile

Post-MBA:
Straightforward Pedigree MBA

(see CASE STUDY 12)

Recruiter's Perspective
- Top 5 business school
- Has end-to-end deal skills — closed, lead, negotiated and monitored deals
- Industry focused
- Well-rounded
- A complete package

Pluses

Nominated by senior management...*Devised improvements to...Selected* by peers to speak... Captain MS Walk Team...Captain United Way Campaign

experience

2001-2004   LARGE PE FUND   NEW YORK, NY

Associate. Responsibilities included evaluating new deals, leading business and industry due diligence, raising debt financing to support transactions, negotiating financing and transaction agreements and monitoring portfolio companies. Industry experience includes Media & Telecom and Industrial & Consumer.

- **Selected transactions and portfolio coverage:**
- - $150 MM equity investment in a $1.4 BN LBO.
- - $3 MM equity investment in digital cable network. Target investment of $20 MM.
- - $40 MM mezzanine investment in owner/operator of mid-market TV stations.
- - $35 MM equity investment in broadband services provider. Served as a Director.
- - $25 MM equity investment in acquisition vehicle in the B2B publishing space.
- **Other:**
- - Formed investment thesis and identified investment candidates in digital cable.
- - Actively reviewed investment opportunities in the business process outsourcing ("BPO") space.

1995–1997   ABC SECURITIES INC.   NEW YORK, NY

Analyst – Leveraged Finance Group. Performed valuation and credit analysis for leveraged buy-outs of companies in the media, industrial and consumer services industries. Presented to internal credit committees, drafted securities offering memoranda and worked with syndications desk to structure and sell underwritten debt securities. Consistently ranked at top of my class.

- Lead-managed several senior and subordinated debt issuances for various acquisitions.
- Nominated by senior management to serve on internal analyst leadership council. Devised improvements to the investment banking analyst program.

Other   **INTERNET COMPANY (June-July 2000)** Member of the team responsible for launch of new product category. Created and presented category business plan to senior management team.

VC FIRM (August 2000) Reviewed early stage investments in BPO, call center and software services industries for $160 million venture capital fund.

OFFICE OF CONGRESSMAN (July-August 1997, Washington, DC). Organized small-business conference in Congressman's home district.

education

1999–2001   TOP 5 BUSINESS SCHOOL

Master in Business Administration degree.

1991–1995   TOP 10 UNIVERSITY

Bachelor of Arts degree in Economics. Dean's List. Received Dean's Awards for student leadership. Selected by peers to speak at graduation exercises.

personal   Lived in India, Japan and Hong Kong. Interests include world affairs, entrepreneurship and golf.

service   Captain – MS Walk Team, raising $50,000 to find a cure for Multiple Sclerosis.

Captain – United Way Campaign, raising $250,000 for various United Way charities.

Profile
Post MBA: A Banker Who Went After The Job In Person
(see CASE STUDY 17)

experience:

summer 2001 | **BULGE BRACKET Investment Bank** | TOKYO, JAPAN

Associate, Investment Banking Division/Equity Capital Markets

Hired directly by senior executive to assist in helping local associates and analysts to develop a broad repertoire of industry skill sets including; valuation, presentation techniques, work ethic and morale.

1998 - 2000 | **Analyst, Mergers & Acquisitions** | NEW YORK, NY

Executed and marketed a variety of M&A transactions. *Offered an Associate position.*

Selected Transaction Execution Experience:

- Senior analyst on a team advising leading Latin American telecommunications company in the formation of a $4.0 billion joint venture with other regional companies. Complex technical analysis involved valuing many disparate assets within four segments (mobile, cable, CLEC and internet) from four different countries.

- Lead analyst on a team advising European company on a $500m bid for Latin American iron ore producer. Managed day-to-day activities reporting directly to a Vice-President. Responsible for extensive client interaction, significant due diligence, complex valuation analysis, detailed minority shareholder buyout scenarios and an understanding of relevant country takeover regulations.

education:

2000 - 2002 | **TOP 5 BUSINESS SCHOOL**

Master in Business Administration degree, June 2002.

1994 - 1998 | **TOP 100 UNIVERSITY**

Bachelor of Science degree, *magna cum laude*, in Business Administration. Finance and Economics concentration.

- 1996-1998: Elected captain of school's development ski team.
- 1995: Overseas University: Completed summer program.
- 1997: Completed a 2-month summer seminar on Finance and International Business in England.

personal: Fluent in Polish. Proficient in Spanish. Internationally ranked alpine ski racer (90-98). Enjoy adventure sports.

community:
- Assisted a $2BN Foundation in developing its private equity diversification strategy.
- Worked with a European city's bid to host the Winter Olympics.

Resume 13

Profile
Post-MBA: Taking A Pre-MBA Role As An MBA
(see CASE STUDY 18)

THE RESUME

WORK EXPERIENCE

6/03-8/03 **BULGE BRACKET INVESTMENT BANK** San Francisco, CA

Summer Associate, Investment Banking (Offered permanent employment)
- Executed $1.1BN secondary offering for major hardware company, including diligence and positioning.
- Evaluated strategic alternatives for a leading semiconductor company on a retained assignment.
- Analyzed debt restructuring options for a regional radio/TV company and a large clothing company.
- Advised a late stage telecom technology start up on options regarding a sale of the company vs. an IPO.

7/99-7/02 **MID-TIER M&A BOUTIQUE** San Francisco, CA

Analyst, Global Technology Group, Investment Banking **New York, NY**
- Executed M&A and corporate finance transactions, including diligence, valuation, positioning, document drafting and financial analysis.
- Established firm's client presence in the U.S. software sector, including screening, establishing contact and developing client relations with over 100 software companies.
- Co-head of West Coast Analyst recruiting and active participant in Associate recruiting.
- Started as the only analyst of the San Francisco Technology Group, supporting up to 7 senior bankers.
- Ranked at the top of the analyst class.
- Informally offered associate position – elected to attend business school.

6/98-9/98 **THE ABC INDUSTRIAL COMPANY**

Intern/Analyst, Strategic Management Center (Offered permanent employment)
- Researched data and created Excel model on the worldwide bearing industry to resolve anti-trust issues.
- Constructed a "toolkit" manual to systematize company's acquisition processes.

EDUCATION

8/02-6/04 **TOP 5 BUSINESS SCHOOL**

Master in Business Administration with Distinction
- Awarded 1st and 2nd Year Honors.
- Elected Treasurer of Squash and Tennis Club and of Volleyball Club.
- GMAT: 770.

9/95-6/99 **TOP 5 UNIVERSITY**

Bachelor of Science in Physics with Distinction and Minor in Economics
- GPA Overall: 3.98; GPA in Major: 3.92; GPA in Minor: 4.24 (A+ = 4.3).
- Phi Beta Kappa inductee.
- Member of Varsity Team (NCAA Champions in 1996, 1997 and 1998).
- Recipient of Student Scholar Athlete Award, 1997.
- In-depth course study: Physics, Mathematics, Economics, Pre-Medical (Chemistry, Biology).

OTHER
- High school valedictorian
- Fluent in Excel, Word, Access and Powerpoint.
- Enjoy tennis, volleyball, football, hiking, skiing, and social dancing.

Profile
VC: A Traditional MBA VC Hire
(see CASE STUDY 25)

THE RESUME

Education   1998 - 2002   **Top 50 University**
- B.S., **Electrical Engineering**
- GPA: 3.6
- SAT: M-800, V-800
- Spring 2002 – Japan (Study Abroad)

Work Experience   2002 - 2004   **Major Consulting Company**
ASSOCIATE CONSULTANT
Strategic and management consulting. Served clients across retail, automotive, construction products, travel services, and real estate.
- Real Estate Investment Trust, Full Potential Diagnostic
  - Identified and collected data on several property performance metrics across portfolio of large multi-family REIT.
  - Used multivariable regression to compensate for market / asset differences between properties.
  - Identified over $100M in revenue enhancement opportunity through internal benchmarking.
- Glass Manufacturer, Growth Strategy
  - Conducted a bottoms-up market sizing and segmentation of the glass industry to guide client in making sales force and product development investment decisions.
  - Identified up to $34M in potential revenue growth opportunities within client's existing product and geographic footprint.
- Travel Services Provider, Growth Strategy
  - Performed win/loss analysis to understand client's relative ability to win proposals in different industries. Insights used to refocus sales force towards selling to selected industries.
  - Developed cash flow forecasting model to assess client's ability to meet revolver terms given varying operating or financing scenarios.
  - Auto Parts Manufacturer, Portfolio Strategy
  - Created financial fact base comparing profitability of client's product lines produced in nearly 30 manufacturing facilities globally.
  - Factbase used for best-demonstrated practice analysis and determination of core products and processes.

Summer 2001   **Investment Bank**
INFORMATION TECHNOLOGY INTERN
- Created a project management application for the network infrastructure division using Java Server Pages with an Oracle database
- Gained knowledge of the financial services industry through classes on derivatives and options and through ad hoc interaction with traders

Summer 2000   **IBM Corporation**
INTERN
- Worked with four technical interns and one MBA intern to develop a location based services strategy for wireless devices
- Submitted two patent applications for a location aggregation framework developed during the summer

Activities
- Junior Achievement
- Formula SAE Powertrain Lead (Build and race auto group)
- Symphony violinist

Honors
Chancellor's Scholar (Campus Honors Program), Mechanical Engineering Outstanding Scholar, National Merit Scholar

Resume 15

Profile
VC: A Consultant With
A Law Degree Gets In

(see CASE STUDY 26)

EXPERIENCE

Major Consulting Firm, *Associate*, New York   Summer 2001; 2002 - 2004

Led complex strategic issue diagnosis and problem-solving, developed strategic recommendations, and managed client teams across multiple functions, including customer acquisition, operations, global organization, sales and marketing, and capability building. Specific examples include:

- Identified, developed, and piloted alternative pharmaceutical sales force models to reach underserved physician segments for major global pharmaceutical company
- Led development of European country strategy for major U.S. pharmaceutical company facing complex competitive challenges to its most important drug. Identified 35 million Euros in incremental revenue through novel positioning
- Developed global R&D strategy for major pharmaceutical company. Wrote business plan to maximize the value of the biologics in support of the larger R&D efforts of the organization
- Built growth strategy for home equity business of major credit card organization. Identified $5-6 million in incremental revenue through customer acquisition strategies and better prioritization of internal resources
- Assisted client to identify opportunities for a start up private equity fund focused on health care
- Conducted training for 2003 associates and analysts; actively involved in interviewing, recruiting
- Selected as Evaluator for National Business Plan Competition for Nonprofit Organizations; served on Nonprofit Leadership Group to encourage Firm interest and commitment to nonprofit work

EDUCATION

TOP LAW SCHOOL, J.D., *cum laude*   June 2002

Activities:	Served as Course Assistant	
Internships:	Law Firm (London, England)	Law Firm (Tel Aviv, Israel)
	Law Firm (New York, NY)	U.S. Attorney's Office (Anywhere, USA)
	Attorney General's Office (Anywhere, USA)	Law Firm (Anywhere, USA)

TOP 5 UNIVERSITY, B.A., *cum laude*, in Economics and Philosophy   June 1997

Honors: Distinction in the Major, Economics; Distinction in the Major, Philosophy

MILITARY   Served in infantry brigade of Israeli Defense Forces (Nov 1998 – Feb 2000). Awarded distinction "Mofet Plugati" as most outstanding soldier during basic and advanced training and tour of duty

MEMBERSHIPS   New York Bar Association (attorney in good standing); Asia Society

chapter XI

THE INTERVIEW

At this point, you've read our insight into the hiring process at PE/LBO and VC funds, learned about the importance of fit and should know how to put together a strong resume. But, the most crucial part of the process is still ahead—the interview. You should not underestimate the value attached to the interviews and the importance of preparing thoroughly for them. You may be a top banker or consultant and know your deals and/or projects inside and out, but for better or worse a large part of business is still about the "human element" and one-on-one interaction. If you don't perform well in your face-to-face interviews, you may never get a chance to showcase your skills at a PE fund.

No matter how you cut it, your interview process will be exhausting and thorough. And that holds true regardless of the size of fund at which you're interviewing, the stage at which it invests or the role for which you're being considered. To help you prepare, this chapter goes over the types of questions that will be asked and the subjects that will be covered during interviews for both later-stage PE/LBO and early-stage venture capital positions. We also devote a good deal of time to discussing the actual structure and timing of interviews because knowing what to expect will help you avoid any surprises and arrive to each round well prepared. Finally, we present some general tips that apply to interviews at all types of funds.

Throughout this guide we've emphasized that funds are looking to hire superior candidates who can help them earn solid returns while also protecting their brand and reputation. Even a $100 million fund will want a star. Remember, the people who started these funds worked hard to get where they are. They are proven achievers and top performers and want the same type of people working for them and the way they size you up in interviews is not too different from the due diligence they do on their own investments. In essence, they want to know if you will be a good investment for them—both in terms of time and money. The interview is your chance to prove that you have more than just the technical skills to excel in the role. Most industry veterans will tell you PE is still a people business and the deals they do are about more than just numbers. A lot of deals (and business in general) are still based on relationships and trust. In that context, you must convince your interviewers that you can be trusted to handle senior level relationships such as putting you in front of the CEO of a company or running a call with an accountant or lawyer.

Later-Stage PE/LBO Interviews

PE/LBO deals are generally more financially complex and there are a lot more moving parts on each deal than earlier-stage deals. Because of this, your interviewers will want to see that you have the skills to handle that type of work. You should expect that initial interviews will often focus on confirming your deal mechanics (usually financial modeling and valuation skills). Questions about hard skills will be an especially big part of pre-MBA interviews, but for all levels there is still more to the equation. Most funds are collegial, close-knit groups and are looking for someone who will work well with them in a collaborative environment. They will use the interviews to get a feel for whether they like you and how well they think you will interact with professionals at the firm, their vendors and executives at their portfolio companies. Your maturity, communications skills, presence and leadership all play a significant part in the people side of the business.

THE PACE

The type of firm and the time of year at which you are interviewing will generally determine the pace of your process. Over the past few years the pre- and post-MBA interview cycles have become more similar. Top pre-MBA Analysts and top-MBAs are both pursued aggressively early in the process (June-September for pre-MBAs and early in the second semester for MBAs) by the larger PE funds with pre-determined hiring needs.

Glocap Insight

A byproduct of the interview cycle is how quickly you may be expected to respond to an offer. PE firms that interview earlier in the cycle can either give candidates the luxury of a week to accept an offer or force their hands and demand a more immediate answer. If you get an offer later in the cycle, however, in nearly all cases you will have up to a few days to make a decision because at that point the candidate pools are thin and hiring firms will not want to be left in the lurch while you make up your mind.

In the case of pre-MBAs, the funds will try to meet as many of the top candidates as they can and quickly advance the best ones to the next round. If a fund is not based in your local area but is interested in meeting candidates in your city, it may fly a few members of its team in to conduct interviews in person. It's best to be flexible around their calendar as they may not make another trip for first round interviews and your one window of opportunity could close. Some funds may also conduct first round interviews via telephone if a face-to-face meeting cannot be arranged (we offer some guidance on phone interviews later in this chapter). First round interviews for MBAs could be on or close to campus. Later rounds will typically be at the fund's offices.

As we explained in more detail in Chapters IV and V, in addition to the top pre-MBA Analysts and the top pedigree MBAs, each year other very qualified Analysts and MBAs get into PE funds. These candidates will most likely interview with PE funds that recruit later in the season as they have less predictable hiring needs and, thus, choose to wait out either the pre- or current-MBA cycle. For both pools of candidates, interviews may be on more of a rolling basis.

If you are a pre-MBA or a current MBA and are interviewing later in the cycle, most PE firms will wonder why you have not been hired yet. They may ask you point blank why you're still available. The reasons can vary, but you should be prepared with a clean story as to why you are still in play. Maybe you were out of the country, maybe you were stuck day and night working on deals, maybe you were offered a couple of opportunities but turned them down because they weren't the investment style you were seeking or they were not in a city that you wanted to move to, or your gut said it wasn't the best platform and you could do better. Perhaps you made a bunch of final rounds, but got no offers. All of those are legitimate responses, however, if you went on 10 first round interviews and were not invited back for any second rounds this raises caution flags and recruiters and employees will try to sniff it out so you should be prepared with a good confident answer if that is the case.

HOW MANY ROUNDS

In general interviews at PE/LBO funds should stretch out over three to four rounds. In the early rounds of most pre-MBA interviews, there will be a mix of penetrating questions to determine quantitative (modeling) and qualitative (big picture/strategy) skills. If you're invited back for later rounds there will probably be more of the same questions, but they may come from different people. Often these rounds become a test of endurance to see how well you can stay engaged and come up with consistent, intelligent answers, while still showing that you are sincerely interested in working at the fund. The middle rounds are those during which the firm is narrowing down the group of candidates according to best fit. For example, funds that use recruiters to prescreen pre-MBA candidates often have 20 candidates in for first rounds, invite 10 back for second rounds and narrow that to five candidates for a final round (of which they may hire one to three people). The middle rounds are also when candidates may decide whether to continue interviewing at a specific fund.

Unlike pre-MBAs, current or post-MBAs won't necessarily be interviewed by junior people, at least not at the beginning. Instead, you will most likely initially meet with people at your level or more senior and the theme will most likely be assessing whether you are Partner track quality. There is a chance that you will be asked to meet one or more junior investment professionals in one of the middle rounds. This may be part of the screening process, so we would suggest not letting your guard down if it happens. We have seen people get dinged because they talked down to someone.

> *Insider Tip*
>
> ## PE ASSOCIATE
>
> "In interviews I generally look for traits that will enable candidates to excel within our environment, because, while our fund may be large, there are really only a few senior managing directors and myself. The ability to learn quickly, to prosper without much supervision and to execute efficiently is highly valued. These abilities are not limited to the type of investment bank one may have been trained at; instead, they are specific to the person and their ability to communicate their strengths/skills to others."

The later rounds are when all candidates should expect to meet the Partners of the fund. In a large firm this may mean just the Partner(s) in the industry group with which you are interviewing. Once you meet the Partners you should be beyond most of the quantitative hurdles so you can expect the interview to be more conversational and qualitative in nature (how you think about investments, etc.). But don't be surprised if you are still asked a few technical questions to spot check your knowledge and see if you are prepared. Partners may also want to re-affirm your interest in them. If you've gotten this far it's probably because everyone else you've met thinks you have the hard skills to do the job and that you can fit into the team and represent the firm and they have probably told the Partner as much. This last step is your opportunity to show the Partners that they were right and you do belong with the firm.

THE "WHY PE" QUESTION

You wouldn't think we would have to tell you, but, you will very likely be asked, "Why do you want a job in private equity?" For those who have already worked in PE, you may be asked, "Why are you pursuing a *career* in PE?" In fact, you can expect almost all the people you meet during each of the different rounds to inquire about this in some form. For many funds a logical follow-up question would be, "Why do you want to work at our fund?" The PE funds want to see that you are genuinely interested in PE, that you have the right motivation for wanting to be in the industry (and at their firm) and that you can express that in a cohesive and articulate way. These are such obvious questions, but you would be surprised how many people bomb them. We've heard of pre-MBAs answering the "Why PE?" question with responses like, "Everyone else in my Analyst class is doing it, so I thought I would too," "I thought it would help me get into business school" and "I want to be on the buy-side." The answer they were hoping for is more likely that you have a passion for investing and that you want to apply your skill set to working hands-on with companies, building businesses and creating value. The following quote from Case Study 3 captures what we are trying to say (note this person came from a consulting background):

> "Go into interviews with confidence and determination. Show them that you know WHY you want to be in private equity and, more specifically, WHY you want to work for them. These are all extremely small organizations where every person is an important member of the team. It's similar to an athletic team with only a handful of members—come draft day, they want to know that you will be a good "draft pick" for them."

DEAL SKILLS

Your financial knowledge and deal skills are always going to be important and you should be able to talk about both. The extent to which you should know your deals and your roles on them takes on different meaning for pre-MBA, current MBA and post-MBA candidates.

Insider Tip

PARTNER AT A PE FIRM

"The biggest mistake made by people interviewing for PE jobs is that they don't take a view. When you are asked, 'What do you think about this investment opportunity?' you have to have an answer. Your view may be wrong, but that doesn't matter if it is well thought out. That's what investing is all about."

Pre-MBAs will be expected to know their models and what went into creating them. At this level, PE/LBO funds are known for asking modeling-intensive questions relating to valuation. We frequently hear that candidates are asked how to calculate "free cash flow." Although this calculation is done by most banking Analysts every day, many have trouble doing it on the spot. The funds will also want to know that you can put together complex models that come up with accurate valuations and that you understand how all financial statements interact. You should be ready to first walk your interviewers through how you construct a model and then be ready to put one together as part of the interview process (though this would not likely happen until a middle round when the hiring fund is more invested in you). In most cases, candidates are told of modeling tests in advance.

If that happens it's possible you will spend a few hours at the fund's offices during your interview (often in a separate room) building a model (you will be given a calculator, a couple of 10ks and whatever else you need). Your performance on this exercise could help determine if you get to final rounds and meet the Partners. It could also be the last indicator of whether you should get the job offer.

Although in most cases pre-MBAs will not be expected to know more than what they did on a particular deal, you can set yourself apart by being able to discuss more dimensions. For example, knowing why the deal was beneficial or not and what the value drivers were, would differentiate you from other candidates. If you worked on a merger, you should know why the companies merged and be able to explain the big picture behind the deal. But be careful. At the end of the day, you're being interviewed for a position that will require intense modeling work, so having A+ answers to the "why questions" will not make up for B+ modeling skills.

Although Case Study 10 appeared in the post-MBA chapter, there is some valuable advice about pre-MBA interviewing, most notably the modeling questions:

> "I interviewed at about 15-20 firms. They all pretty much asked the same questions: How do you get to free cash flow? Walk me through an LBO that you worked on. How would you model it? They grilled me on my deals asking if I thought they were good ones—basically anything on my resume was fair game. I think this is a weak point for people with banking backgrounds. They are used to burying themselves in the models. They have to learn to take a step back and judge the entire deal. Some gave me quantitative brain teasers and all asked why do you want to go into PE? I would also add that since the PE firms don't train you they will expect that you got your training from your Analyst program and they will test that during the interviews."

For further proof of the lengths PE firms will go to test your modeling skills, take a look at what the author of Case Study 1 had to say. In his case, some of the modeling questions even came from Partners. As you may recall, this person began pre-MBA interviewing in late summer and in the space of a few weeks had his offer in hand:

> "I would advise other banking Analysts interested in PE to be sure they want to do it well before the recruiting period comes up. You've got to go after it hard so you better want it and do your homework, especially when it comes to preparing for interviews. It sounds obvious to say that you better know your LBO models and your deals inside and out, but it's true. On my interviews I was grilled pretty hard by the Partners. The firm that eventually extended me an offer had me meet just about everyone that I would be working with, that meant about 12-15 people. About half of them asked me about my work and the others just wanted to get to know me and see if I would fit in with the firm. All the other firms asked me pretty technical questions. They asked me to walk them through an LBO model. Some would show me an LBO model and say, 'Let's say the depreciation changes by $1 million, talk about how every line in your model changes.'"

For current and post-MBAs, the finance/modeling questions will not be as intense. If you worked previously in PE you may be asked some basic questions to test your knowledge, but for the most part the funds will assume that you have the quantitative skills to do the job. If you get a job you would not be putting together as many models, but you will have to understand the models that others produce. Candidates should be well-versed in discussing origination, due diligence/valuation, negotiations/structuring, interaction with management and any operational/strategic work that went into deals.

If you are a current MBA even though it was two years ago, you will probably start off being quizzed about the pre-MBA PE/LBO deals on which you worked and specifically on your responsibilities. The funds will then probe to see whether you were superior to people at your same level, that you were further up the curve and that you took initiative. However, at this level, what they really want is to gauge your Partner track skills which can include things like comfortably interacting with senior management, having deal sourcing ideas/skills and understanding deal strategy. They want to know what you learned, who you learned it from and with whom you worked. For example, was it just you and a Partner on deals?

PERSONALITY MATTERS

Although we spoke at length about fit in Chapter IX, we feel it's important to point out that interviews are when your personality and potential to fit in with the culture of a fund will be scrutinized. Not only does personality and cultural fit matter, but we've found that firms are often highly stringent in assessing these points. You may have had a good enough resume to get an interview, but your ability to fit in—and the hiring firm's impression of whether you will—becomes a big differentiator on whether you will get an offer.

As recruiters, more than half of our time is spent assessing the qualitative skills and personality of a candidate to determine if they should be sent on an interview. It's easy to determine from a resume if a candidate has the pedigree and hard skills required. Our clients, however, also hire us to send them someone who we think will mesh well with their team. PE funds will be feeling you out throughout the interview process to see if you are a good fit for their firm. Remember, even though they may control hundreds of millions of dollars in investments, these are relatively small firms (even the very large ones with several billion dollars in assets under management may only have 50 people and some billion dollar funds can have as few as a dozen investment professionals) so the Partners and other investment professionals want to feel comfortable working and interacting with you.

In addition to simply speaking with you, we estimate that 10-20% of firms go as far as giving candidates personality assessment tests—the Myers-Briggs Type Indicator is the most common. These tests, which most often are given after the final round, are designed to define personality types that help hiring firms determine how well certain people will interact and serve as a double-check against potential conflicts. We have found that the hiring firms that use these tests put a lot of weight on the results and your performance on them can weed you out even after you have met everyone.

CASE STUDIES/TESTS

Case studies/tests are frequently part of the interview process. If you know what's coming you could prepare (like building a model), however many PE firms want to see how you react on the spot. The cases/tests are usually designed to measure your thought process to see if you are insightful and resourceful and to see how you work under pressure. Therefore, we warn you to expect surprises. For some you may be given a few days to review a business plan and put together an analysis and valuation as part of a PowerPoint presentation that you will present to a mock investment committee (see Case Study 13). We have heard of one PE fund that put a candidate in a room with a stack of industry publications and gave him a couple of hours to identify some investment leads and to present an argument as to why they were good investments.

DO YOUR HOMEWORK

All candidates should research the firm and the professionals they will be meeting. Initially, that means knowing what the fund does. This may be obvious, but funds still complain to us that people don't do enough research. We think at a minimum you should know the fund's size, how long it has been around, the stage at which it invests and its investor base. You should also familiarize yourself with recent deals the fund has closed. While you're looking at the portfolio companies, it wouldn't hurt to pick two or three and assess, in your opinion, why they were good investments for that fund and how they mesh with the fund's investment strategy. You should also know the larger market and have some investment ideas so you can be prepared for any case studies.

You should also be familiar with the backgrounds of the investment professionals, including the schools they attended, where they're from (if you can find that) and the consulting firms, banks or companies at which they worked prior to joining the fund. Knowing their professional backgrounds can give you some insight into the style of interviewing that you can expect (consultants and bankers are known for asking specific types of questions). Most funds have detailed web sites, so getting this information should be relatively painless. Not having it is almost inexcusable.

To reaffirm what we are saying, take another look at the interview advice in Case Study 7 from someone who beat the odds and got into PE directly out of undergrad:

> "Before interviewing, I networked with alumni from the firm who gave me a sense of what to expect. Most private equity firms have Web sites where they give extensive information on their investments and the backgrounds of the people. I walked in with info on every person, thoughts on potential areas for investment, and opinions and questions on recent deals the firm had done. That gave me a lot to talk about in meetings and I think probably stuck out. Finally, having a clear, credible story on why I wanted to be in private equity was critical, and being able to back it up with experiences on my resume showed I was serious."

Insider Tip

PE PRINCIPAL

"You'd be surprised how many candidates come unprepared to an interview at my firm. We will often ask, 'what's an investment we've made recently and why do you think it or its industry is interesting, or not?' The stuff is right on our web site, but people don't look. As a banker the same person would never go to a client meeting unprepared. It is a pleasure to interview someone who is well prepared, because it makes for an interesting meeting and because you know they will bring that same approach to the job."

INTERVIEWING FOR A SOURCING ROLE

Some funds bring on junior professionals for deal sourcing roles. These are quality roles and many successful firms utilize Associates in this way. These are generally positions that require a lot of cold calling and/or business development. They are most often at a growth equity or venture capital fund and have gotten more popular as the competition for deals has increased. In these positions valuation/modeling skills are less of a focus. We usually recommend people interviewing for those positions try to identify a few private companies that would be good investment opportunities and be prepared to talk about them in their interview—this is almost always a direct question that you will be asked. You may also be asked to prepare a 10-minute presentation complete with slides that would be given to companies explaining why they should partner with the fund at which you are interviewing. This, of course, is also a test of how much you know about the fund, its past investments and its strategy.

SOME ADDITIONAL ADVICE FOR CURRENT MBAs

There are several nuances specifically related to MBA interviewing worth highlighting. In Chapter V we pointed out that the hiring market separates MBAs into two camps—those with and those without previous PE experience. We also noted that those who worked in PE pre-MBA have a distinct advantage landing positions when they graduate and, therefore, our advice was different for MBAs in each group. As you would expect, the process and questions asked during interviews for MBAs with and without prior PE experience differ as well. Below are some specific points for MBAs to keep in mind.

If you have prior PE experience and want to return to the same type of investing you were doing before business school you can expect a pretty straightforward interview. For example, if you did middle-market consumer LBOs and want to continue on that path you should know exactly what to say. But if you want to change fund profiles, you need to effectively explain why the transition makes sense for you and how the hiring firm will benefit from your past experience. For example, if you were doing domestic tech investments and want to do cross-border manufacturing deals, you will have to put together a strong case.

The same goes for any change in stage of investment, for example, if you have venture experience, why would LBOs now make sense? You should also be ready to explain your choice of a summer job during business school since that sends signals about the direction in which you are going. Case Study 11 gives a good look at one person's MBA interview experience:

> "Most of the interviews were pretty similar and I would say that people should be prepared. Only one firm gave me a case to read and prepare notes. The rest would have me walk through my background; ask about what deals I had worked on, why I wanted to work in PE and why with that specific firm. The fact that I had worked at a hedge fund in the summer, but was seeking a job in PE also came up at every interview. Some also asked questions like, 'If you had money to invest, where would you put it?'"

In general, if you are not returning to your pre-MBA PE firm you can expect to be asked why that is the case. You should have a solid, unwavering, non-abrasive answer prepared to share in interviews. Many candidates stumble over this. Saying, "The fund is not hiring anyone" is easy, but, if they are bringing back others, why are you not one of them? If you didn't think it would work out, avoid sounding disgruntled. If you say it was your choice, the funds will dig deeper to make sure. You need to convince them to make them comfortable. If you can't explain why you are a better candidate than when you entered business school, you will not impress your interviewers. On the other hand, if you do well at conveying how you have grown into a better investor then the odds are good that there will still be a spot for you.

If you are a current MBA and don't have PE experience, you can't rattle off previous successful investments you were a part of. So if you do get an interview your investment judgment, financial knowledge and deal skills will be scrutinized instead. There's no hiding the fact that you don't have a PE background, so you will have to work extra hard to convince a fund that you created value in the past and can do the same for them. One way to do that is to define a situation in which you helped create value or added to the success of a project or deal. Maybe you helped launch a new product, turned around a troubled division and/or got a deeper understanding of business, management and operations issues. It will also be helpful to talk about any superior achievements you've had whether they are professional, athletic or academic.

Venture Capital Interviews

If you've read Chapter VIII, you know that venture investing is very different than later-stage PE/LBO investing, so it's natural that the interviews will be too. These differences were pointed out well by the author of Case Study 25 who interviewed at both types of funds:

> "There was a stark difference between the interviews at buyout and VC funds. The buyout Partners grilled me on financial matters, asking me the different ways that I might structure a deal, what different sources of funding I might use and when I would use one over the other. VCs asked more goal-type questions than skill-testing questions. I was asked why do you want to be an investor? What stage of investing do you like? What types of companies do you like? I know one venture fund that gave candidates an assignment to evaluate a company by coming back with a PowerPoint presentation and model."

THE PROCESS

Similar to PE/LBO funds, the interview process at VC funds typically lasts about three to four rounds, but the pace of the process from first to last round can be different for pre- and post-MBAs. At the pre-MBA level, candidates can expect a quicker and more structured interview process as those VC funds that do hire at this level compete for some of the same bankers and consultants as the PE/LBO funds and therefore have to also match their timing. At the post-MBA level, the hiring is typically done with a lot less urgency. In fact, in Chapter VIII, we pointed out that VC funds rarely actually "need" someone at this level and that can make interviews play out for several months.

The experience of the author in Case Study 27 gives some good insight into post- MBA interviews (he joined his VC fund after nine years in operations):

> "The interview process took about six months and the firm seemed in no hurry to bring someone on. I met with everyone on the investment team and was asked things like: What did you learn while at the start-up? What areas do you think are promising to invest in? How would you evaluate investment opportunities?"

By their nature, most VC funds are small firms and don't have as many layers as PE/LBO funds. Thus, you could meet Partners very early on in the process. It's also possible that you will meet the same people multiple times and it's a good bet that each person will ask you similar questions to see that you have a strong understanding of business and technology and that you combine that with solid commercial instincts. In one of the middle- to later-rounds you may be given an in-depth case study (we discuss those more in a bit).

For post-MBAs, interviews in the mid- to later-rounds could include evaluating a live deal or even visiting a potential company with the deal team. By going to this length the VC fund is treating you as it would a member of its investment team and seeing how you would perform in such a situation. When that meeting is over, most of the hard core testing will have been completed. At this point, your last meeting could be a dinner with the Partners which may also involve significant others.

To prepare for VC interviews we suggest all candidates—pre-MBA and post-MBA—learn as much as possible about the funds and the investment professionals who they will be meeting. In most cases, the fund's Web sites can provide a lot of what you need, but you should supplement that information by speaking with people in the business including other venture capitalists and even recruiters. Being familiar with the investment professionals and the Partners includes knowing where they went to school and where they worked prior to venture—for example, do they come from a banking, consulting or operations background?

Given the availability of information, it's inexcusable not to be fully informed about the VC fund where you are interviewing. Knowing the industry in which the fund invests and being able to talk about it is a start. After that, you should also know the fund's major investments—the winners and the losers—and the overall venture capital market so you can put the fund and its investments into context.

THE "WHY VC" QUESTION

Initially—possibly in the first round—VC funds will ask why you want to be a venture capitalist and why you want to work at their particular fund. That may seem obvious, but you should have an answer ready. As described in Case Study 24:

> "The most important thing is to be passionate about venture. You should not be in it for the money and should definitely not come off as if you are. If you are passionate, curious and excited then you will want to learn the science and finance. And, the passion should not just be for venture, it should be for venture, biotech (in my case) and being an entrepreneur."

We've heard of people answering the "Why do you want to work in venture?" question by saying something like, "I want to take companies public." That may sound good, but it's not necessarily what an Associate would be doing. Another mistake would be to say that you want to do valuation work (remember, VCs don't utilize those skills in-depth). What they would rather hear is that you have a deep passion for technology or life sciences and that you want to apply that to being a strong investor. They want to feel your enthusiasm for discovering new products and developing ideas that could re-shape a specific industry and that you will work tirelessly to successfully develop those ideas and products into successful companies.

OTHER QUESTIONS

In general, interviews at VC funds will focus on your business sense and your overall market knowledge. You will be asked what you did in past jobs and how those experiences can help the fund earn returns. The VC funds are worried less about the mechanics of what you worked on, but they do want to know your thought process and where you believe there are opportunities. Since a good part of your job will be evaluating business plans they will want to know how you recognize value in start-up companies.

Your interviewers will want to see that you understand the sector in which the fund invests and that you have thoughts on where that market is headed. For example, if you're coming from an operations background, you will be asked what the market is like for the products you worked on, what technology you used and how that market is evolving. Ideally, you will have ideas about which companies in the industry you worked are possible investments. If you are a consultant you will be asked to walk through your projects. It's important that you have opinions on the projects and explain your role and your input.

After assessing your industry expertise, VC funds will also want to know that you are familiar with the players in the specific industry and if you have a network to access interesting companies. Needless to say, if you are not already familiar with the companies in your space of expertise we recommend you get acquainted with them. As we explained in Chapter VIII, you may have the deep industry expertise required by a VC fund, but if you are not familiar with the terminology used in the venture community you could appear weaker on a relative basis to others who do know this. In that case, we recommend you become familiar with terms such as "Series A and B" financings, "up and down rounds," "pre- and post-money" valuations and "Angel funding," etc.

Don't be surprised if a fund specifically tests your industry knowledge. For example, if you say you know software you might be asked to identify an enterprise software company worthy of investment. VC funds want to confirm that you are on top of major trends on both macro and micro levels. As you talk you should demonstrate your familiarity with the emerging companies and technologies within the industry. A more probing question might be how you would determine the value/potential of a specific company or business plan in the absence of financial statements. As a follow-up you could be presented with the following question: "If you're given a stack of 25 business plans what would make one jump out at you?" You may even be asked something like, "If you had $1 million what would you do?" "In which industry would you invest?"

You will more than likely be asked if you invest your own money in the stock market and to explain the thought process behind those investments. We've even heard of funds asking questions such as, "If you had all your life savings invested in one stock, which would it be and why?" Again, they want to see what you look for in a company and how you evaluate investment ideas. At the very least they want to understand your ability to assess risk/return and that you have confidence to act on your position.

Most industry veterans would agree that the venture business is still driven mainly by people. There are two aspects to the people side of the business—the VCs need to like and trust their colleagues and the people running their portfolio companies. As small partnerships VC funds are like a marriage so how you get along with the other professionals on the team is important. Therefore many of your interviews (even if you are not aware of it) will be to see if you are a fit for the firm.

CASE STUDIES/TESTS

Formal case studies are a big part of VC interviews. As either a pre- or post-MBA a large majority of your time will be spent sourcing, screening and qualifying deals for the Partners and involves reading a lot of business plans. Case studies can either be written or verbal and could be take home or an on-the-spot presentation. We know of VC funds that present candidates with a company that it had considered as a possible investment. In such a situation, you may be told what issues and/or reservations the fund had with the company and then you will be asked how you would evaluate it. The fund wants to see if you think like an investor. You may get to take the business plan home with you and come back in 48 hours with a more thorough presentation. The VCs want to see that you are a good thinker and problem solver.

General Tips

Below are a few miscellaneous suggestions that everyone should keep in mind regardless of whether they are interviewing at an early-stage venture capital, growth equity or a leveraged buyout fund:

PHONE INTERVIEWS

Some funds may conduct the first 1-2 rounds of interviews over the phone. In this case you should prepare in the same manner as if they were in person. These funds know they will not decide to give an offer to a candidate solely based on a phone interview—but most are willing to eliminate candidates based on this screen. If a fund likes you, they might respond by saying, "We really enjoyed speaking with you. Let us know the next time you will be in town so we can meet in person." This generally means that the plane ticket will be on your dime.

OUT OF TOWN INTERVIEWS

Someone who really wants a job and is given a soft offer for an in-person interview like the one mentioned above will figure out a way to make that meeting. To us the smart candidates distinguish themselves by finding creative ways to get in front of a firm (many clients use that as a natural selection tool to see who is more driven). Maybe they re-route a return flight from a business trip or make a point to be in a specific city to see family, visit friends or combine a trip with other interviews. Since there are still no guarantees that funds will not cancel at the last minute, there is some inherent risk in just showing up—but maybe having to assess that is a good screen for a future investor. In our view, a blind trip for the interview is not usually wise, unless you truly are prepared for it to be cancelled and, if that happens, you cannot feel burned or complain.

DRESS CODE

Even though most PE firms are known for being business casual, our advice is to always play it safe: when in doubt, wear a suit. For women that means a full suit with jacket and either pants or skirt. You will never be penalized for being over-dressed, but you could lose points for dressing inappropriately. We'd also caution men about their selection of neckwear. We're not saying that a certain tie will get you the job, but you probably have one in your wardrobe that should be avoided. The only time we would say that it is acceptable not to wear a suit is if a recruiter tells you that it has been cleared with the firm where you have an interview. And, even in that case we recommend you avoid wrinkled clothes, or rolled-up sleeves. Keep it clean and conservative. We have never heard of earning points for creative dressing in a PE/VC interview, but we have heard of points being deducted.

BE ON YOUR BEST BEHAVIOR

There are some firms that go out of their way to wine and dine finalist candidates (this is especially relevant with pre-MBAs). We know of one that will fly you to their offices for a Friday interview and have you stay the weekend so you can see if you would like living in that city and we have heard of other firms doing similar things. It should go without saying, but we'll point out anyway that you should always maintain a level of professionalism during interviews, group dinners and casual outings sponsored by the hiring firm. You should basically assume that you are on a 24/7 interview. Therefore, avoid saying something too casual, beginning inappropriate conversations on taboo topics such as politics. Do not drink too much and watch your language. The people interviewing and hosting you are not your friends (at least not yet) and you should not act as if they are. Believe it or not, each year we get feedback on a few candidates losing an imminent offer for some of these reasons, so playing it safe is usually the default option.

chapter XII

COMPENSATION

We assume that compensation is at least *part* of the reason you want
to work in private equity, but we hope there are other reasons that
are equally as important. Since profits in private equity are realized
over the life of a fund—often 5-10 years—don't expect to hit pay dirt
early on. For most professionals, the first few years of compensation
will be driven mainly by base salaries and cash bonuses. Don't get us
wrong, you can do well with your annual base and bonus, but this is
not investment banking where annual bonuses are typically your one
big payday and where, even as an Associate, after a strong year that
bonus can be multiples of your base salary. In PE the big money
comes further down the line in the form of carry when a fund is successful and is bringing in profits from its investments.

Executives at all private equity firms frequently tell us they want people who understand the longer investment cycles of PE and are ready to put in the work to reap the benefits down the road. If you truly want
a long-term career in PE, you have to exude that mindset because staying with a fund and building up
equity—known as carried interest—are the best ways to accumulate wealth (we offer a more detailed discussion of carry later on). If you look at any ranking of top-earners in private equity, those at the head of
the list are not there because they have high salaries. Of the people on the 2006 Forbes list of the 400 rich-
est Americans, 13 are there based on fortunes made from leveraged buyouts and/or venture capital. We
can safely assume that their fortunes were earned because they produced tremendous, consistent value over
long periods of time by having the patience and discipline to make successful investments and reap the
high equity returns.

We generally believe that a higher offer from one fund doesn't necessarily mean it is the better offer. Each
year we see candidates turn down more short-term cash for various tradeoffs including a better promotional track, more professional growth, increased responsibilities or, of course, upside potential in terms of
equity. The bottom line for candidates is that if you are joining a smart team with a strong investment
platform and if you understand the long-term investment cycle, your compensation should work out in
the end.

PRIVATE EQUITY VS. HEDGE FUNDS

Since private equity and hedge funds compete for some of the same talent, it's important that you understand the compensation structure of each type of firm. In Chapter I, we explained that PE funds are not
affected as much by short-term fluctuations in the stock market as are hedge funds. In contrast to PE,

which is more of a long-term equity game, hedge funds are marked-to-market each year and bonuses are calculated based on annual profits. PE is not for people who are overly concerned with earning a lot year one. If you get restless about making money at your current fund and think the solution is to make a lateral move, be careful. Chances are you will have to prove yourself again to re-establish goodwill with the new team. In some cases, that could mean taking a step back economically. We have seen some people benefit economically by making a switch, but have seen others who built up equity at one firm and are happy they did not make a contemplated move. Either way, you should know how your compensation will be affected if you do change firms.

VENTURE CAPITAL

As we pointed out in Chapter VIII, venture capital is different in many ways from later stage PE/LBO and that extends to how VC funds pay as well. Total cash compensation at VC funds is lower than it is at similarly sized PE/LBO funds. It should be noted, however, that VC funds, on average, can pay higher base salaries than do PE/LBO funds, but those salaries usually represent the majority of total compensation. The differences in compensation are attributable in part to the inherent differences in how venture capital and PE/LBO funds invest and the role of non-Partners. PE/LBO funds are very focused on adding value through the deal itself and non-Partners are paid a premium (in the form of hefty bonuses) to be part of closing complex transactions. Success in venture investing is more driven by Partners growing portfolio companies and non-Partners typically have less involvement and ultimately less impact on the eventual success of individual deals. That's not to say you can't make a lot of money in venture capital. Although, total compensation will be lower in the beginning (before you become Partner) there is no question that venture capital offers great prospects for long-term wealth creation (assuming investment success) that can be equal to (or even greater than) that of PE/LBO and hedge funds.

COMPENSATION TRENDS

Compensation ranges for Analysts, Associates and Vice Presidents can vary substantially and are driven by asset class and fund size and in turn the management fees earned. The chart below gives a more detailed

CHART 8
2007 Compensation Breakdown By Job Title *(all fund sizes)*

		Private Equity	Venture Capital	Fund of Funds
Analyst	Average Base Salary	78k	74k	71k
	Average Bonus	75k	46k	37k
	Total Cash Compensation	153k	120k	108k
Associate	Average Base Salary	90k	106k	88k
	Average Bonus	89k	52k	50k
	Total Cash Compensation	179k	158k	138k
Sr. Assoc.	Average Base Salary	142k	128k	136k
	Average Bonus	147k	70k	60k
	Total Cash Compensation	289k	198k	196k
VP	Average Base Salary	182k	174k	163k
	Average Bonus	222k	110k	86k
	Total Cash Compensation	404k	284k	249k

Source: The 2007 Private Equity Compensation Report
Note: The data does not include compensation from carried interest.

breakdown of average base salaries and bonuses at funds of funds, private equity and venture capital firms (see Chapter I for a definition of each type of fund). The figures are all averages based on data compiled for the 2007 Private Equity Compensation Report and include all fund sizes.

In addition to Chart 8, we have some compensation figures to give more specific guidance. In today's highly competitive market large PE/LBO funds (those with at least $3.5 billion in assets under management) may offer top-tier MBAs annualized total cash compensation packages of $400,000 (base salary plus bonus) and higher. The superstar pre-MBA Analysts and Associates, who are those people fresh out of their two-year investment banking and consulting programs, are being offered packages at the large PE/LBO firms that can total $200,000 or more in their first year and even more in the second year (the norm is probably $160,000-$190,000).

Over the past year, we have found that the increases in PE compensation were driven primarily by the larger average fund size and the competition for top talent both among other PE/LBO funds and from hedge funds. These factors are especially evident given the record-breaking year for PE fundraising. The influx of new cash has increased the need for talented people, while the increased management fees have allowed the PE/LBO funds to pay for that talent. Hedge funds have also been targeting the same group of candidates, putting additional upward pressure on compensation. Although the increase is most prevalent among the mega PE/LBO funds (those with more than $3.5 billion) it has trickled down through the rest of the industry.

The 2007 Private Equity Compensation Report illustrates that even the *average* cash compensation in PE is significant. Total compensation for Senior Associates (those fresh out of business school) at PE funds with $1.5-$3.5 billion in assets under management hit a healthy $327,000. Although VC funds pay higher base salaries, the total packages (base salary plus cash bonus) are lower than those at PE funds with average total compensation for Senior Associates at large venture capital firms ($1.5 billion and above) hitting $254,000, according to the 2007 report. We believe that total cash compensation across the industry should continue to increase as the robust fundraising, coupled with competition for talent, show no signs of slowing.

CARRY

Those people striving to get into the PE industry should understand the role of "carried interest." Carried interest is the portion of fund returns that are paid to the General Partner, which as we pointed out in Chapter I, can range from 15-30% of profits (20% is most common). This is the General Partners' fee for carrying the management responsibility plus all the liability for providing the needed expertise to successfully manage investments. There are many ways to calculate this profit share (in dollars, points of fund carry, or percent of fund carry) and to account for it. Carried interest is an integral component of overall compensation and, just like receiving stock in a company, the vesting schedules can vary (ranges are generally three to eight years). We have noticed that the percentage of overall carry earmarked for non-Partners has steadily increased. We estimate five to 10 years ago, about 85% of the carry was held by the Partners. In today's market, however, we believe 75-80% is more common. We have also noticed that of the non-Partner carry, close to one-half is allocated to the next generation of leaders (usually at the Principal level). From our experience, approximately 80% of funds offer newly minted MBAs a percentage of carry.

chapter XIII

Working With A Recruiter

Some candidates complete a successful job search on their own, but many find working with a recruiter who specializes in private equity to be beneficial.

As recruiters, a large part of what we do is reaching out to candidates. If you're a first year pre-MBA Analyst at an investment bank or consulting firm or if you are nearing the end of your first year in business school and have previous private equity experience you can expect to get calls from a recruiter when the PE hiring season begins—for top Analysts that could be as early as April or May and for graduating MBAs it could be just as the second year of business school begins. If you're a star banker, meaning you're in the top of your Analyst class you may get calls from multiple recruiters. Either way, it will be up to you to decide if the recruiters are calling with the jobs you want. For those of you whose phone doesn't ring, it doesn't mean that you're out of luck. You may simply be in a less visible/sought after geography or be in a less-recognized banking or consulting program in which case you may want to reach out to recruiters yourself.

We're often asked by candidates how we decide who to invite in for a meeting after receiving their resume. We typically agree to meet candidates who have the right resume variables for our clients so we can then determine if you have the right non-resume variables (e.g., personality, demeanor, communication skills, etc.). Therefore, the best way to get in front of us is to make sure you have the relevant industry experience (investment banking or consulting for pre-MBAs and private equity for post-MBAs) and a strong academic background at both undergraduate and graduate levels (if applicable).

If you don't have the relevant industry background that a PE recruiter is looking for, then securing an interview with that recruiter will be tougher. In this situation we'd strongly suggest using your personal network (get recommended to the recruiter by somebody we know and respect) or persistence (to a point). In our case, a personal recommendation carries a lot more weight if it comes directly from someone we know well in the PE world. For example, rather than an e-mail from you saying, "Joe said I should give you a call" it would be helpful if Joe e-mailed us with, "I know someone who I think you should meet. His background may not be perfect, but he's a great guy, knows his stuff and has what it takes."

Depending on the level of position and the competitive landscape we estimate that approximately 30-50% of PE professional roles are filled by recruiters. In an industry such as PE there historically has not been a

RECRUITERS

shortage of high-quality people and therefore a recruiter is often hired not only to find candidates for a client but just as importantly to screen candidates for the optimal fit and caliber.

Tips For Getting The Most Out Of A Recruiter

MAKE THE INTRO

Introduce yourself briefly—this can be by e-mail or phone (for Glocap you would register on our Web site). As we said, if you can get a high-end recommendation you will likely fare better. In a recruiter interview, you should start with a few sentences describing your background and highlight your major strengths. Explain why you are looking to leave your current position and note your potential job interests. Do not re-state your entire resume. If applicable, mention how you got the recruiter's name (referred by a colleague, etc.).

WE'LL CALL IF WE SEE A MATCH

Professional recruiters will usually respond to a direct inquiry from you as a courtesy. The response could be via e-mail, or a quick call back. You'll likely receive a call as well if your background is a good match for a particular client with whom we are *currently* working. If the recruiter doesn't have any opportunities to discuss with you they might still want to connect to learn more about your background for future reference or will simply hold on to your information until a search opens that does match your background.

NO PRACTICE INTERVIEWS

If you're presented an opportunity, be honest about your level of interest. If it's your dream job or your qualifications match the job perfectly, explain that to the recruiter—it could help them better market your background. If you haven't heard of the firm or need to contemplate the opportunity further, feel free to take a few days to research and think it over. Do not take the interview for practice, informational purposes, etc. Recruiters are sensitive to wasting their client's time. If you decide to pass on an interview briefly explain why and perhaps have a follow up conversation to hone in further on your job search interests.

RECRUITERS AS RESOURCES

Think of recruiters as a valuable resource. They may have additional insight into a particular firm and position, which could help you evaluate the opportunity and prepare for an interview. A good recruiter who spends enough time getting to know you as well as their client is in a great position to find the all-important "fit." Recruiters are usually entrenched in the market, so, as we explained in Chapter IX, a recruiter could be a good source of information about how a fund is perceived in the market. We are happy to give advice to many candidates even if we do not place them.

GIVE FEEDBACK

After a client interview, let the recruiter know how your meeting went and if you're still interested in the position or would like to bow out of the process. Be specific about how the opportunity does or does not meet your interests. It's fair to ask if the recruiter has received feedback as well. Most recruiters will share constructive feedback they've received from the client but please, don't shoot the messenger!

KEEP US IN THE LOOP

Stay in touch with your recruiter if your search criteria have changed at all, if you're approaching final rounds at another firm, if you were recently promoted, or if there were other general changes in your profile. When checking in with a recruiter, be specific. If you'd like to inquire about the status of a certain job, note the firm's name or job/reference number. Try to avoid touching base "in general"—this usually adds little to no value to the recruiter or your job search.

RECRUITERS

KNOW WHAT YOU WANT

Most successful candidates are specifically focused on what they want. It's OK to have job interests in several different areas provided your skill set really does extend that far, but try to tier your interests and identify which opportunities are most interesting and fitting for you.

DON'T PLAY HARD TO GET

Be responsive. If you're contacted by a recruiter make a point to follow up as quickly as possible. If you're slow to respond they may think you are uninterested, out of the market, or even difficult to represent. Remember, you need to make a good first impression on the recruiter in order to be introduced to their client.

HIRING FIRMS HAVE THE FINAL WORD

Our clients (the hiring firms) are the ones who pay recruiting fees. As such they can define as narrowly as they please the set of resumes and backgrounds that they are interested in seeing from a recruiter. The question is not whether you can learn the job, but rather if you have the background that the client wants. While you may be a 75% fit for the job, someone else could be a 98% fit and you just may not stack up competitively enough. And, even if you do check all the boxes there may be others applying for the same position who also check those same boxes but are even more qualified.

NO ATTITUDE PLEASE

Remember that you are one of many candidates with whom the recruiter is working. You can certainly feel confident about being a strong candidate, but having an attitude that conveys, "You will make money off of me" is not a good way to get the attention you want. A wise recruiter knows that a great candidate can also be a potential future client. When working with a recruiter, your job search is a collaborative effort!

RECRUITERS

Appendix

News Publications/Trade Journals

There are many publications and Web sites that cover the private equity industry. These are always a good resource and can help you stay abreast of fundraising efforts both for existing and newly formed funds as well as hiring updates. A lot of the newsletters and Web sites have job listings, but reading about new funds can be an equally effective way to find out about potential opportunities. Similarly, stories about people being hired and moving from one fund to another can give insight into the backgrounds sought by specific funds or, better yet, leads about potential vacancies. These stories could also help you research funds at which you have interviews.

Private Equity Analyst
www.privateequityanalyst.com

Private Equity Week
www.privateequityweek.com
*You can sign up for PE Week Wire,
a free daily update.*

Private Equity Insider
www.peinsider.com

Private Equity Central
www.privateequitycentral.net

Private Equity Online
www.privateequityonline.com

Financial News Online
www.efinancialnews.com

Buyouts Newsletter
www.buyoutsnewsletter.com

The Deal and The Daily Deal
www.thedeal.com

European Venture Capital Journal
www.evcj.com

Venture Capital Journal
www.venturecapitaljournal.net

Suggested Books

PE/LBO

Barbarians at the Gate: The Fall of RJR Nabisco
by Bryan Burrough

*Buyout: The Insider's Guide to Buying
Your Own Company*
by Rick Rickerstein, Robert E. Gunther &
Michael Lewis

Den of Thieves
By James B. Stewart

*The New Financial Capitalists: Kohlberg Kravis
Roberts and the Creation of Corporate Value*
by George P. Baker & George David Smith

*The Predators' Ball: The Inside Story of Drexel
Burnham and the Rise of the Junk Bond Raiders*
By Connie Bruck

VENTURE CAPITAL

*Deal Terms – The Finer Points of Venture Capital
Deal Structures, Valuations, Term Sheets, Stock
Options and Getting Deals Done*
by Alex Wilmerding

APPENDIX

eBoys
By Randall E. Stross

Fundamentals of Venture Capital
by Joseph W. Bartlett

Inside The Minds: The Ways of the VC
Aspatore Books

*The Money of Invention, How Venture
Capital Creates New Wealth*
by Paul A. Gompers & Josh Lerner

The VC Way
By Jeffrey Sygment

Venture Capital and Private Equity: A Casebook
By Josh Lerner

*Winning Angels, The 7 Fundamentals of
Early Stage Investing*
By David Amis & Howard Stevenson

Directories/Glossaries

Galante's Venture Capital & Private Equity
Directory, published by Asset Alternatives Inc.
www.assetnews.com/products/dir/galante.htm

The Directory of Venture Capital & Private
Equity Firms, Grey House Publishing
www.greyhouse.com/venture.htm

Glossary of Private Equity and Venture Capital
vcexperts.com/vce/library/encyclopedia/
glossary.asp

Venture Economics Private Equity and
Venture Capital Database
www.ventureeconomics.com
> *Venture Economics, a unit of Securities Data
> Corporation, provides profiles of firms backed
> by venture capital and buyout funds in its
> VentureXpert Database. It also provides informa-
> tion about the amount of and the investors in
> each financing round.*

National Venture Capital Member Directory
http://www.nvca.com/members.html

vFinance Venture Capital Resource Directory
www.vfinance.com/ventcap.htm

Privateequity.com Private Equity Database
http://www.privateequity.com

The PSEPS Venture Capital and
Private Equity Directory
http://www.private-equity.org.uk/

Academic/Business School Clubs

The New York University:
The Stern Private Equity Club
http://pages.stern.nyu.edu/~spec/index.html

The Center for Venture Capital and Private
Equity Finance at the Stephen M. Ross School of
Business at the University of Michigan.
www.bus.umich.edu/CVP/index.html

The Tuck Private Equity Club at the Tuck School
of Business at Dartmouth
http://mba.tuck.dartmouth.edu/pages/clubs/pecl
ub/index.html

Wharton Private Equity Club
www.wharton-pec.org

Harvard Venture Capital & Private Equity Club
http://sa.hbs.edu/vc/

Yale School of Management Private Equity
Student Interest Group
http://students.som.yale.edu/sigs/private_equity/

Other Resources

American Venture Network (www.avce.com)
Publishes American Venture Magazine
www.americanventuremagazine.com

Private Equity Info
www.privateequityinfo.com
Subscription-based source for information on private equity firms—their investment interests, portfolio companies, and professional biographies. Has a regularly updated database of firms and contacts.

Private Equity Intelligence
www.prequin.com
Information on products and services for private equity funds, venture capital funds, funds-of-funds, investors and advisors. Contains fund performance, investor profiles, fundraising and research and consulting information.

The American Entrepreneurs for Economic Growth
www.aeeg.org
AEEG is the affiliate organization of the National Venture Capital Association. It is the largest nationwide network of emerging growth companies that focuses on public policy issues impacting rapidly growing enterprises.

Regional U.S. Venture Capital/Private Equity Associations

Colorado Venture Capital Association
www.coloradovca.org

Connecticut Venture Group
www.ct-venture.org

Dallas/Ft. Worth Private Equity Forum
Contact pfh1521@aol.com.
Evergreen Venture Capital Association
www.evca.net

Florida Venture Forum
www.floridaventureforum.org

Greater Philadelphia Venture Group
www.gpvg.com

Illinois Venture Capital Association
www.illinoisvc.org

Long Island Capital Alliance
www.licapital.org

The Mid-Atlantic Venture Association
www.mava.org

Missouri Venture Forum
www.missouriventureforum.org

Minnesota Venture Capital Association
www.mnvca.org

New York Private Equity Network
www.nypen.net

Venture Investors Association of New York
www.viany.org

San Diego Venture Group
www.sdvg.org

Venture Club of Louisville
www.ventureclub-louisville.org

The Western Association of Venture Capitalists
www.wavc.net

Young Venture Capital Association
www.yvca.net

Young Venture Capital Society
www.yvcs.org

Non-U.S. Venture Capital/Private Equity Associations

Australia Venture Capital Association
www.avcal.com.au

Austrian Equity and Venture Capital
Organisation
www.avco.at

Belgian Venturing Associations
www.bvassociation,org

Brazilian Venture Capital Association
www.abcr-venture.com.br/english

British Venture Capital Association
www.bvca.co.uk

Canadian Venture Capital Association
www.cvca.ca

China Venture Capital Association
www.cvca.com.hk

Czech Venture Capital Association
www.cvca.cz

Danish Venture Capital Association
www.dvca.dk

Emerging Markets Private Equity Association
www.empea.net

European Venture Capital Association
www.evca.com

Finnish Venture Capital Association
www.fvca.fi

Association Francaise des Investisseurs en Capital
www.afic.assoc.fr

German Venture Capital Association
www.bvk-ev.de

Gulf Venture Capital Association
www.gulfvca.org

Hong Kong Venture Capital Association
www.hkvca.com.hk

Hungary Venture Capital &
Private Equity Association
www.hvca.hu

Icelandic Venture Capital Association
www.efa.is

Irish Venture Capital Association
www.ivca.ie

Israel Venture Association
www.iva.co.il

Italian Private Equity and
Venture Capital Association
www.aifi.it

Japan Venture Capital Association
www.jvca.jp/en

Malaysian Venture Capital Association
www.mvca.org,my

Netherlands Venture Capital Association
www.nvp.nl

New Zealand Venture Capital Association Inc.
www.nzvca.co.nz

Norwegian Venture Capital Association
www.nvca.no

Poland Equity Investors Association
www.ei.com.pl

Philippine Venture Capital Investment Group
www.philvencap.com

Associacao Portuguesa De Capital De Risco
www.apcri.pt

Russian Venture Capital Association
www.rvca.ru

Slovak Venture Capital Association
www.saef.sk

Singapore Venture Capital and
Private Equity Association
www.svca.org.sg

South Africa Venture Capital &
Private Equity Association
www.savca.co.za

Spanish Venture Capital Association
www.ascri.org

Swedish Venture Capital Association
www.vencap.se

Swiss Private Equity &
Corporate Finance Association
www.seca.ch

Thai Venture Capital Association
www.venturecapital.or.th

Turkish Venture Capital Association
www.turkvca.org

Glocap Search is an executive search firm focused on the alternative asset industry and has a global practice placing investment professionals at all levels from General Partners down to Analysts into private equity funds. It also has substantial practices placing CFOs, Controllers, COOs, Admin/Support, IT, and Marketing professionals into these same funds.

With over 100 recruiters and offices in the U.S. and abroad, Glocap is one of the leading search firms serving the alternative asset community. Glocap's dedicated, specialized teams of search consultants have all worked in the industry into which they place or from which they draw their candidates and have similar educational pedigree. This insider position and the level of knowledge that comes with it, gives us the ability to work in close partnership with clients to understand in depth their needs, culture and internal processes. In many cases, in addition to placing professionals for our clients, we act as a trusted advisor on compensation trends, optimal organizational structure and competitive landscape.

WWW.GLOCAP.COM

About the Author

BRIAN KORB

Brian helped co-found Glocap Search and is currently Head of the Private Equity Practice. Brian oversees several aspects of Glocap's Executive Recruiting division and personally works on placing experienced senior investment professionals into select Private Equity/LBO and Venture Capital funds. From his experience covering the Private Equity industry since 1997, Brian has developed a deep insight into emerging compensation and hiring trends that he uses to advise clients looking to shape their core staffing/growth strategies. Brian graduated with a B.S. in Economics from The Wharton School with concentrations in Finance and Accounting.

Contributors

AARON FINKEL

Aaron is Glocap's Vice President and Head of Publications. He is an experienced financial writer and editor having spent over a dozen years as a reporter and editor with Institutional Investor's newsletters. He has written extensively on emerging markets, corporate finance, private equity, venture capital, asset management and compliance. In addition to overseeing Glocap's annual Private Equity and Hedge Fund Compensation Reports, Aaron is creating a series of Glocap employment guides, of which this is the first. Aaron graduated from Brandeis University.

LANDON SPITALNIK

Landon is Vice President of Business Development. Prior to joining Glocap, Landon was with Alesius Capital, an alternative investment advisory firm that he co-founded. Previously he spent three years doing direct private equity investing at Three Cities Research. Landon graduated from The Wharton School at the University of Pennsylvania with a BS in Economics and concentrations in Finance and Entrepreneurial Management.

We would also like to thank the private equity and industry executives who spoke with us and whose quotes are used throughout this guide as Insider Tips and the many investment professionals who shared their job-search stories with us in the form of Case Studies.